T0353714

The Racial Justice Series
By
Roberto Schiraldi

~

Healing Love Poems
for white supremacy culture:
Living Our Values

Unexpurgated*Racial Justice Poetry
with Healing Meditations

Men and Racism:
The Healing Path

Multicultural Counseling
with Boys and Men:
A Healing Guide

Post Traumatic Macho Disorder
The Way Home

Multicultural Counseling With Boys and Men:
A Healing Guide

ROBERTO SCHIRALDI

BALBOA.PRESS
A DIVISION OF HAY HOUSE

Scripture quotation taken from the Holy Bible, NEW INTERNATIONAL VERSION®, NIV® Copyright © 1973, 1978, 1984, 2011 by Biblica, Inc.® Used by permission. All rights reserved worldwide.

Balboa Press books may be ordered through booksellers or by contacting:

Balboa Press
A Division of Hay House
1663 Liberty Drive
Bloomington, IN 47403
www.balboapress.com
844-682-1282

Because of the dynamic nature of the Internet, any web addresses or links contained in this book may have changed since publication and may no longer be valid. The views expressed in this work are solely those of the author and do not necessarily reflect the views of the publisher, and the publisher hereby disclaims any responsibility for them.

The author of this book does not dispense medical advice or prescribe the use of any technique as a form of treatment for physical, emotional, or medical problems without the advice of a physician, either directly or indirectly. The intent of the author is only to offer information of a general nature to help you in your quest for emotional and spiritual well-being. In the event you use any of the information in this book for yourself, which is your constitutional right, the author and the publisher assume no responsibility for your actions.

Any people depicted in stock imagery provided by Getty Images are models, and such images are being used for illustrative purposes only. Certain stock imagery © Getty Images.

Print information available on the last page.

ISBN: 979-8-7652-5833-0 (sc)
ISBN: 979-8-7652-6025-8 (hc)
ISBN: 979-8-7652-5832-3 (e)

Library of Congress Control Number: 2024926332

Balboa Press rev. date: 02/13/2025

Contents

Prelude vii

Dedication ix

Gratitude xi

Preface xiii

Introduction xv

The Heart of This Work

A Letter Of Appreciation For You...My New
    Counselor Friend 1

Mitakuye Oyasin / Some background 4

Multicultural Counseling In A Culture of Fear:
    A Journey Through Alienation and Privilege
    to Healing 11

Values 24

Values Meditation and Prayer 29

Moral Inventory and Valuing Process 30

Men and Racism / Considerations and Strategies... 32

White Heterosexual Male Privilege. Why every
    counselor should feel comfortable discussing it.... 42

Healing From The Trauma Of Racism 49

Mental health and wealthy white hetero male
    supremacy culture....the Dilemma 55

Broaching 60

To Broach (for a counselor) 63

The Ethics of Broaching 65

Holding Space For Transformation and
    Communicating Non-Violently 68

Calling Out / Calling In 71

Double Jeopardy! 74

Outline for Core Curriculum Course 80

New Jersey Counseling Association Anti-
    Racism Statement * 116

American Counseling Association / Anti-
    Racism Statement 119

Racial Justice Pledge 122

Initial Strategies For Engaging in Racial Justice
    Work 123

Justice Healing Meditation 126

Men for Racial Healing and Justice Proposal 128

White Supremacy as Addiction/Twelve Step
    Recovery 132

All Life is Sacred 136

Healing From Pain 166

Heart of the Pain Soothing Mediation 168

Closing and Hope 171

Author Contact Info 173

Prelude

Physician Heal Thyself

...........Please.

Dedication

To Dr. Mark Woodford,
For your outstanding long term commitment
to training so many new counselors
about multicultural counseling
and helping our boys and men to heal

Thankyou for inspiring me to write this book

Gratitude

To My Loving Partner Eileen
For teaching me to be a better man,
And your unwavering support of my
Racial Justice and Healing work.

Preface

Many years ago I was asked to give a presentation at a local university medical school. "Physician Heal Thyself" was the theme.

We in the "mental health" field would do well to heed that call....especially when it comes to <u>healing the dis-eases of racism</u>....and all the other isms....sexism, homophobia, classism, xenophobia...that live inside each of us.....from growing and living in a world rampant with hurtful, biases and discriminatory behavior.

Many of us have made a life long commitment to "doing our own work"........many of us...have not.......... which can lead to further hurting ourselves, our clients, and those we say we love. <u>Unfortunately...extensive multicultural counseling training........(taking deep dives into the wealthy white hetero male supremacy cultural values that we have all been continuously exposed to.... and uncovering the huge impact on our lives, and how we work with our clients).... is not required of all counselors. It definitely should be. It is unethical that it isn't. The standard CEU's requirements for licensure and renewal in generic diversity training....is woefully inadequate to address such a critical issue...that deeply hurts so many of our clients.....so many of us. To do counseling work</u>

with folks who have been racially traumatized....when we have not done our own work....can re-traumatize our clients.

What is offered here are some of the most basic and essential ingredients of multicultural counseling ..for boys and men....which I believe should be at the forefront of all counselor training...especially since it effects so many of our mental health problems.

We are all in great need of more extensive training and ongoing support in this important multicultural self healing work, as well as how to provide similar support for our clients. Many of us men, especially, have all too few healthy role models, and inadequate training in how to be healthy people.

Thank you for caring enough to explore this further.

Introduction

While this Guide is particularly offered for all counselors who work with boys and men, and multicultural counseling, it can be helpful to all who care about healing themselves and helping our world to be a better place.

Helping ourselves and each other in healing from the wounds of racism...and all the other hurtful discriminatory effects and affects of sexism, homophobia, classism, xenophobia ...is a challenging, yet life affirming practice.

Since my primary life's work has been as a trauma therapist.....and racial justice advocate....I decided to offer this for all my colleagues, friends, and allies in the healing field. Most of the articles and other pieces herein have been borrowed from my previous racial justice healing books.

Being committed to healing myself, and supporting others in healing themselves.... it is my deep hope that you find this helpful with your own healing work, and the healing of your counseling clients and loved ones.

THE HEART OF
THIS WORK

A Letter Of Appreciation For You...
My New Counselor Friend

Dear Fellow Counselor,

Welcome! Thank you for choosing to do this important work. I honor and respect your decision. Why you made this decision is of course extremely important. And I know that some of you, especially if you are in a graduate counseling program, might still be deciding if this is right for you. So I honor and respect you for looking honestly at why, and if this is a good match for you.

As you well know, while there is so much goodness and beauty in this world.....there are also so many of our fellow humans who are in pain and suffering, and greatly in need of support.

As many of you already know....this can be incredibly gratifying and fulfilling work........

.....and also.... excruciatingly difficult, challenging, even painful.

So providing support for those who are hurting....in this case, <u>boys and men...and regarding racial trauma and multi-cultural related concerns</u>... can bring with it's own set of gifts and challenges. It is therefore very important that we learn all we can about boys and men and multicultural concerns, as well as, and perhaps, even more importantly....how it impacts on us. How do we feel about what we think we know, what we don't know, and how does our life experience relate or not relate to who and what we are engaging with.

This is why it is so vital that as I said in the intro.... we "do our own work", before trying to "save" anyone else....lest we do more harm than good.

And hopefully, "doing our own work", especially engaging in our own counseling as needed, will be a life long process. This, along with our supervision, continuing education, colleague support, counseling associations ....and hopefully involvement with racial justice advocacy...will best ensure that we are forever growing, and learning, and re-learning our life lessons, so that we may be the healthiest and happiest we may be......in order to optimally support our clients in being the same.

I have been very blessed to be able to make a living... from doing something that I "love" so much. My clients have been great gifts for me...as they often inspire and teach me by their commitments to healing.

I feel very grateful to have found help for myself, many, many years ago..when I was hurting and not sure if I wanted to go on. Sure glad I decided to commit to learning how to love myself, so that I could share those gifts with others.

So I offer these articles, poems and other pieces which follow.

May you find some of what you're looking for here.

Roberto

Mitakuye Oyasin / Some background

I started writing poems back in 1969 while stationed at the army hospital, waiting for the choppers to come in that we'd unload with stretchers of the wounded, amputees, and traumatized from Viet Nam. I worked in the intensive care psychiatric unit with those who had PTSD (even though we really didn't have that diagnosis back then). The writing helped me to stay a "little" more sane, while being part of the war machine I detested (having been in the peace movement when I got drafted, and working for the underground publishing letters from other soldiers about the atrocities we were committing over there).

This poem is called Mitakuye Oyasin....which is Lakota for all my relations, all my relatives, we are all connected.....we are all one....

All life is sacred...I was taught this when being blessed to be invited to spend parts of many summers on the Rosebud Reservation in South Dakota, home of the Sicangu, Lakota People, and being a supporter for part of traditional spiritual healing ceremony called Sundance.

Sacred, meaning important, worthwhile, valuable, precious, worthy of love, dignity, respect, awe and

Roberto Schiraldi

wonder....and that all life is sacred.....and I am no better, no worse than that insect, that tree, that child, that woman....and that other man.....all life life is sacred. Imagine how different the world would be if that is the core value we lived by and taught our young ones, especially our boys and young men.

(This poem was part of a keynote for a multicultural counseling conference entitled "Boys to Men" in Multicultural Counseling: Envisioning Change through a Male Lens", November 2014.)

Mitakuye Oyasin / Lakota for All My Relations

A poem to all my relatives
From A white man on the REZ

I feel like
I've never fit in
And that's my only sin.

And to live my truth
need to Speak my truth
That we're each unique..
and each KIN.

My wounds teach me
where I came from,

Scars remind me
to never forget-
So many lessons to learn,
from folks I still haven't met

A song of surviving?
NO...I choose thriving
truth, not lying,
nor continual denying.

They say we're post racial
and let's move past-
I can't, and won't
it's in my bones, my cells, my molecules, my DNA
So healing don't come fast.

How many lifetimes
does it take to heal?
From being the only ones
forced to come here....
and being treated as subhuman, savages, slaves, animals,
property.....
How many lifetimes to heal?

I don't want to forget that truth,
the values, that founded our country are still alive and
well

6   *Roberto Schiraldi*

elitism, power, wealth, control,
entitlement, competition to be #1 at all costs,
white heterosexual male privilege
all values that can create living hell.

I have a mental "dis-order",
that needs to be controlled?
Or is the system what's disordered
and I just don't fit the mold...
of the values that are cold.

If I say I don't see Color,
I'm really saying I'm blind,
to the truth of having a dark skin
and how folks can be so unkind.

If I cut my hair
speak, dress, walk and talk, WHITE,
then, maybe the American Dream will include me,
am I dreaming? Wake UP!!,
they really want me disappearing from sight.

For we can't sing and dance together,
and we can't be truly free,
until we acknowledge the truth,
of what I can't always see,

That we are different,
and we are the same,
and the tragedies
are not about blame.

And the Tyler Clementes, Travon Martins, and Michael
Browns of our country,
will continue to be murdered like dogs,
Until we stop pretending their human,
and admit they're still seen as "hogs".
(from "A Lesson before Dying" by Ernest Gaines, a
young Black man in the 40's South, wrongly convicted
of killing a white woman, after being called a hog by a
prosecuting attorney, said before he was executed, he just
wanted them to know, he wasn't an animal, he's a man.)

Unless we're willing to remember,
what was done to the Indians and slaves,
then we might as well dig us a Hole,
and go back to living in caves.

It's too uncomfortable, you say,
let move on to a brand new day,
not nearly so uncomfortable, I say
as spending a life playing straight,
when I'm gay.

So simply being alive,
Do I deserve a piece of the pie?
Or do I need to prove my worth,
by continuing to live a lie?

Hmmmm.

So what's the answer,
I ask,
It's clear,
No easy task,.

And yet, it's really quite simple,
the wise ones have always taught,
That All life is sacred,
and worth is not earned or bought.

That each of us is born worthy,
and All life is precious and unique.
Yet each of us are also connected
and deep, deep inside is All we seek.

For the greatest power is truly LOVE,
yet rarely is that what's spoken,
in our homes, churches and schools,
in our counseling rooms even a token.

What are we so afraid of,
to be all we truly can be?
By teaching each other bout love
the essence of you and me.

And our boys to men
in each culture,
will Then start, learning and grow,
to be strong and gentle and honest,
and be more than we'll ever know.

So please, My Dear Friends,
please, please look deep inside,
for we each are precious and sacred,
and there is nothing to hide.

For the real adventures
aren't out there.
The real adventures
are home......in here (in our hearts).

So let us embark on this day,
with hope, courage and joy,
And celebrate the backgrounds
we come from,
As we tender the man from the boy.

Mitakuye Oyasin.... Namaste.....Molte Grazie.

Roberto Schiraldi

A White Man on the REZ Multicultural Counseling In A Culture of Fear: A Journey Through Alienation and Privilege to Healing

(The following is excerpted from a longer 14 page article. It is my hope that this will pique your interest to want to read the entire article).

When a White man first enters onto an Indian reservation he may feel like he doesn't belong. Many of our clients also don't feel like they belong when they come to their schools, jobs and communities. While it is clearly not the same, the feeling of being different can certainly raise awareness and sensitivity. This article will examine how as a reflection of a "culture of fear" (given the state of the recessionary economy, poor job market, global warming, terrorism, wars and other social conditions), overt, subtle and often unintentional privilege and discrimination can affect our clients, and how we in the counseling profession can be most supportive in empowering our clients to heal and grow in the midst of these challenging opportunities. A theoretical framework and practical strategies are provided to assist those interested in addressing these issues.

In 2001, I had my first of eight opportunities to spend time on the Rosebud Reservation in South Dakota. Though some of the Lakota people were friendly, I felt a sense of discomfort. The people stared at me in the stores, held their gazes as I drove by, and some even ignored me as I wished them a good morning. It was culture shock. And it hit me hard, that I didn't fit in - - I was a white man on the reservation.

How do many of our schools, work places and communities feel to individuals when they first arrive? Many of our clients, especially those of color, those from different cultural or socio-economic backgrounds, LGBTQ individuals, and individuals with disabilities, quickly feel disenfranchised, disempowered and alienated, feeling like they simply just don't fit in. I believe that one of the primary roles as counselors should be to provide a safe haven where our clients can address these issues.

A white man entering onto a Native American reservation parallels many of our clients entering onto our campuses, workplaces and communities, particularly in the shared experience of being the "other". My experience was certainly a wake-up call for me, a powerful reminder of how it feels to not be part of the norm. However, there are clear differences based on historical and contemporary experiences related to being White, Native, and other racial and ethnic minorities.

The important work of intersectionality theory can be helpful here to better understand these differences. Intersectionality theory examines how there may be many factors which intersect on multiple and often simultaneous levels, thus contributing to systematic and social inequity. These factors may include biological, social and cultural categories such as gender, race, class, economic status, ability, sexual orientation and other measures of identity (Anderson, Collins, 2003).

So too, the experience of feeling different is often not solely based on race, but additional factors which may not be so obvious, such as sexual orientation, culture, and economic status.

For the white man entering the reservation, being the "other" may be an isolated experience. This is especially true if he grew up in a predominantly white, middle class neighborhood and is heterosexual. However there may be white people who are privileged based on their racial status, but disadvantaged due to some other statuses such as being poor, gay or having disability. A sense of marginalization may be more normative for the young Black student entering onto the campus (Cannady, 2009), especially if he grew up in a poor, predominantly

Black neighborhood, and went to a predominantly white high school. The white, heterosexual middle class man may be able to choose to leave the reservation to return to his privileged life. The student of color who is poor may lack that option. If the Black student is lesbian and poor she will likely face additional challenges in fitting in on campus as well as in her culture and community she came from. Thus we can see how many factors can influence the level of privilege and discrimination which individuals may experience.

Given the fast pace of technological change or *Future Shock* (Toffler, 1975), and the state of the recessionary economy, poor job market, global warming, terrorism, wars, and other social conditions, many of our clients, especially younger ones, feel overwhelmed and ill-prepared to make choices that often will affect the rest of their lives. They are trying to find their place in a world that often feels harsh and unwelcoming, a world presenting a "culture of fear". Fear can breed insecurity and the striving for more power, wealth and control to give the illusion of security. Power, wealth and control create privilege, and the more some have, the less other's have. Those who have power, may often stereotype and perceive homogeneity because their perceptions are rarely challenged by those not in power (Fine, 1997; Keltner, 2003). It is a self-perpetuating cycle.

Our schools, workplaces and communities are reflections of the best and worst of the larger culture. Whereas many elements of our culture welcome diversity, others are elitist or discriminatory, or both. Therefore, while usually subtle and often unintentional, these same elements of elitism and discrimination are also present in our schools, workplaces and communities.

Further, there appears to be an exclusive, heightened focus on getting good grades for the purpose of getting good jobs ("not that there's anything wrong with that", as comedian Jerry Seinfeld says). This results in many of our students feeling like their self worth depends solely on their academic performance. I continually hear clients express longing for more warmth and collaboration, rather than cold competition. I believe that the ultimate mission of ourschools, workplaces and communities is to help individuals to develop into healthy, well-balanced (emotionally, mentally, physically, spiritually, socially), happy, responsible citizens of the world. As a reflection of that mission, I believe that our primary goal as counselors is to support our clients in learning how to embrace their core inner worth and of the worth of all living things. A Buddhist teaching is that "the greatest privilege is to know oneself".

In discussing privilege, it is important to emphasize that educating ourselves and our clients about this topic is not about blaming or finding fault, but rather about helping us to increase our understanding and compassion, and creating an environment that is more fully accepting and more fully embracing of all differences.

While there are many forms of privilege, I will here refer to the term white privilege, because I am a White male, because, (1) in this culture, at least, most power, wealth and control still lies in the hands of White men, and (2) because it provides a clear context within which to explore healing. This is not about bashing wealthy White men, or anyone else. For if we have food, clothing and shelter, we have a certain privilege. We can each feel equal, powerful and privileged in given moments. Similarly, we can each feel unequal, powerless and unprivileged in given moments. For example, I can feel equal, powerful and privileged after presenting on white privilege at a national conference and being enthusiastically received. However, I can also feel unequal, powerless and unprivileged when my efforts to address the same topic were met with hesitancy and trepidation at the elite university I was employed by. While this is understandable, given the discomfort this topic can create, it can also feel discouraging.

White privilege may be simply defined as the benefits, such as prestige, power and privilege, derived solely because of the color of our skin, and often at the expense of people who are not white (McIntosh, 1988). Why, when many view the term as offensive and divisive, can it still be helpful to use it? The main reason is that the harmful norms and values inherent in the term "white privilege", are alive and well, that is, elitism, superiority, and competition for power, wealth and control. While these norms and values are not uniquely white, they certainly continue to permeate our culture and our world. And even when the whites in this culture become the minority (which they soon will be), the prevailing white privilege norms and values will continue to be emulated by people of color, women and others who ascend to the power positions. Until these norms and values are replaced by healthier ones, such as inclusion, cooperation and sharing the wealth, using this term can help us to keep our focus on creating change, which will serve all.

While the term, "white privilege", initially may be uncomfortable to acknowledge, it can also be very useful in helping us to better understand how many of the members of our communities often feel marginalized. It is important for us to examine how white norms continue to exist, and how they may hinder people of color from feeling really welcomed in our schools, workplaces and communities. Some very basic examples of white norms are the way people speak, dress and act. If you don't imitate these norms, you don't feel like you fit in. As a counselor, I have heard many painful stories from clients who feel disenfranchised due to their race, gender, ethnicity, sexual orientation, disability or socio-economic status.

One place that individuals can receive support for addressing these issues is in counseling. Acknowledging that we, as counselors, have very rewarding, yet often very difficult and frustrating jobs, is an important starting point. Many of our clients come to us hurting, scared, and confused. Because of heavy case loads, understaffing, and increased need for training, we often feel limited in what we can provide. Sometimes it feels as though we're merely putting band-aids on our clients – so they can go back out to continue the fight. We sometimes feel ill-equipped to handle the increasingly severe levels of anxiety and depression with which we are presented. Medication is prescribed with more frequency, as students are labeled with increasingly serious diagnoses.

Clearly, it is our primary responsibility to provide the best treatment we possibly can with each client we see. And that is a worthy goal. Addressing the emotional, mental, physical, spiritual, and social needs of our clients on a broad scale is a much greater task. Most of us don't have the time or the energy to do outreach, prevention, training and advocate for social change.

The following are some strategies for encouraging us to begin or continue the process of engaging in this important work for ourselves and our clients:

1. **Remember that this can be hard work, that takes a lot of empathy and courage. So it's important to be gentle and compassionate with ourselves. For example, taking lots of deep breaths, and giving ourselves lots of "atta girls" and "atta boys", and breathing in comfort and words of nurturance and encouragement.**

2. **Be willing to continue uncovering our own biases as we continue to work on enhancing our self-awareness (Johnson, 2001), so we can become more comfortable talking about diversity and privilege with peers and students. For example, keep a white privilege journal of reminders and new learnings about our biases and privilege, as we continue to affirm and acknowledge our efforts.**

3. **When appropriate, let our clients know we are open to discussing these issues. For example, have pictures and artifacts in our offices that help make it clear of our sensitivity to**

multicultural issues. When appropriate, share our interest in discussing these issues.

4. <u>Remind our clients, especially our young men, about their internal worth, rather than looking for external validation</u> (Schiraldi, 2001). Help them learn how to celebrate their uniqueness, and of their interconnectedness to all other living things. For example use the crystal picture found in chapter four of Schiraldi's Self-esteem Workbook mentioned above, to demonstrate how our essence is worthiness, however we've often been taught a belief system that focuses on materialism and external validation.

5. Support our clients in learning how to deal with feeling different and disconnected, for example through offering support groups that address related issues such as multi-cultural concerns, <u>being male/teaching our young men how to be gentle with themselves and our world</u> (Kivel, 1993), healthy relationships, and managing emotions, with approaches such as dialectical behavior therapy (Marra, 2005), mindfulness meditation (Kabat-Zinn,1990),and learning how to meet basic human needs such as acceptance, connection, empathy, through learning the art of non-violent

communication (Rosenberg, 2003). **Each of these aforementioned approaches teach specific tools about learning self-respect and emotional management with ourselves and empathetic connection with others.** (*Additional strategies for individual counselors and for addressing these issues on the institutional level, are provided in the full article. To request a copy please contact or email me at robertoschiraldi@yahoo.com).*

When we address inequity, power and privilege we help ourselves and our clients on our healing journeys. May we choose to be kind to ourselves and all our relatives.

References

Anderson, M., & Collins, P.(2003), *Race, Class, Gender: An Anthology.* Michigan: Cengage Learning.

Cannady, E.B., (2009). The African-American College Student Experience: A Qualitative Approach at the University of Wisconsin-La Crosse. MS in Education, 122pp. (L.Ringgenberg).

Fine, M., Weiss, L., Powell, L.C., & Wong, L.M. (1997). *Off White: Readings on race, power and society.* New York: Routledge.

Johnson, A., (2001). *Privilege, Power, and Difference.* New York: McGraw-Hill.

Kabat-Zinn, J. (1990). *Full Catastrophe living.* New York: Delta Publishing.

Keltner, D., Anderson, C., Gruenfeld, D. (2003). *Power, approach, and inhibition.* Psychological Review, 110, 265-284.

Marra, T. (2005). *Dialectical Behavior Therapy in Private Practice: A practical and comprehensive guide.* Oakland: New Harbinger Press.

McIntosh, P. (1988). *White privilege and correspondences through work in women's studies (Working Paper No. 189).* Wellesley, MA: Wellesley College, Center for Research on Women.

Rosenberg, M.B., (2003). *Nonviolent communication: A language of life.* California: PuddleDancer Press.

Schiraldi, G.R., (2001). *The Self-Esteem Workbook.* Oakland: New Harbinger Publications.

Toffler, A., (1974). *Future shock.* New York: Random House.

F. Roberto Schiraldi, EdD, LPC, LCADC

(Three more recent books from individuals I know and highly respect):

Edmond, E, (2024). *Mindful Race Talk: Building Literacy Fluency And Agility.* Connecticut:Mindful and Multicultural Counseling.

Fisher. L (2021). *Diversity in Clinical Practice: A Practical and Shame-Free Guide to Reducing Cultural Offenses and Repairing Cross Cultural Relationships.* Wisconsin: Pesi Publishing.

Hardy, K., *Promoting Cultural Sensitivity in Supervision: A Manual For Practitioners.* New York: Routledge

Values

For each of us, and our clients, choosing to live by <u>clear values</u> is the ticket to real freedom. When we are congruent with our most cherished values...like impeccable integrity, compassion and equity, a lot of our multicultural concerns will be addressed in the most loving ways. And as Victor Frankel so wisely teaches us in his epic inspirational 'Man's Search for Meaning' (when he is facing imminent death in the Nazi gas chambers),....."the only thing we really have any control over...<u>is our attitude</u>"....and with that conviction, no oppressive individuals or systems can really control us.

(The following was used as part of the keynote on "Men and Multicultural Counseling". The belief is that, as we support our boys and men, and all of us, to embrace and live by our most healthy human values, racism will eventually die out).

Values

It's About Values
And Taking A Stand

This being human,
Always a <u>choice</u>.
When to take a stand,
and lend our voice.

<u>Knowing </u>our values
Being firm and clear,
Always a choice,
between love and fear.

So let's see now....

"<u>Unhealthy</u>",
      <u>traditional,</u>
<u>white,</u>
      <u>heterosexual,</u>

<u>masculine,</u>
 <u>supremacy</u>
 <u>values;</u>

competition
 elitism
entitlement
 superiority
power
 wealth
success
 control

Or,

<u>"Healthy",</u>
 <u>traditional,</u>
<u>feminine,</u>
 <u>(and "healthy",</u>
<u>male,</u>
 <u>values:</u>

cooperation
 sharing
generosity
 consideration

nurturance
    kindness
support
    encouragement

And,

"Healthy",
    traditional
human,
    values:

integrity
    dependability
courage
    humility
gentleness
    strength
service
    respect
equity
    patience
compassion.

Alright now...
hope that helps you some
always important to figure
where we're coming from.

Roberto Schiraldi

Values Meditation and Prayer

May we each continually choose to break free from the chains of patriarchy which dehumanize us all.

May we each continually choose to live by our most beautiful loving values.

May we always do our best to listen to that little, still voice of truth inside, which gently guides us home again, to re-member to re-connect with, our grandest version of our greatest vision of who we truly are. The question is always..."What would love do now?...."What would be most loving thing I can do for myself in this situation?" (which will also end up being most loving for the other..even though they might not initially like it, because they're not getting their way.)

(With deep appreciation to Neale Donald Walsch and his 'Conversations With God' books)

To take a values inventory please go to next page. (two other versions of this inventory appear as part of the All Life is Sacred Proposal, later on in this book).

Moral Inventory and Valuing Process

The following inventory was developed by my brother Glenn R. Schiraldi, and adapted by me with his permission. Glenn is a caring teacher and writer about resilience and healing from trauma -

please check out his books and workbooks. The idea here is to take a fair and non-critical look at our character strengths / values, first looking at how we treat ourselves, and then how we treat others. The number 1-10 serves as a guide to what improvements we may wish to make. In general, the valuing process is as follows:

1. Clarifying and understanding, the meaning and implications of each value.
2. Choosing, after carefully considering alternatives and consequences of living each value.
3. Taking action, which consistently reflects chosen values.

Roberto Schiraldi

The Fearless, Searching, Kind Moral Inventory*

No person can be truly at peace with himself if he does not live up to his moral capacity - Norman Cousins**

Character Strength	Rate Yourself from 1-10. 10 means you are living this strength as well as a person can.		Describe a time in the past when you demonstrated this strength		Describe what you could do to demonstrate this strength better and more often.	
	Self	Others	Self	Others	Self	Others
Courage means persisting in doing the right thing despite the pressure to do otherwise.						
Honesty means you speak only the truth, always. No "white lies," half-truths (truth can be tactful and kind), cheating or stealing.						
Integrity means your behaviors match your values and that you show your sincere, authentic self without pretense.						
Respect means you honor people and treat them as worthwhile; are civil and courteous.						
Fairness means you play by the rules, do not take dishonorable advantage of others, and treat others impartially.						
Loyalty, faithfulness, and trustworthiness means you keep commitments and confidences, don't speak ill of others behind their backs; reliable.						
Responsible means able and willing to respond to valid needs and duties; dependable; protects self and others.						
Kind, caring means you are concerned for the welfare of others, desire to help and support their growth; considerate, generous, tenderhearted.						
Sexual integrity means sexual expression is used in the context of love and concern for the other, and never used in a selfish or exploitive way.						
Tolerant means you are patient with differences and imperfections of others; forgiving						

*Reprinted with permission from Schiraldi, G. R. (2011), *The Complete Guide to Resilience: Why It Matters; How to Build and Maintain It*. Ashburn, VA: Resilience Training International. © 2011 Glenn R. Schiraldi, Ph.D.

Men and Racism / Considerations and Strategies

From Keynote / Multicultural Counseling With Males: Adventures in Returning Home"

Initial Considerations/Generalities (disclaimer/ a lot of generalities about men/important to be sensitive to the many differences and distinctions, amongst and within families/cultures:

1. This is not about blaming males. Quite the contrary, it's about empowering boys and men to make a loving difference in our own lives and the world around us.

2. While we males have made and continue to make so many positive contributions to our world, we are also, unfortunately, responsible for contributing to the vast majority of violence, oppression and destruction.

3. Because of the ever increasing amount of anxiety, fear, depression, stress related problems, more and more males are starting to come in for counseling.

Roberto Schiraldi

4. Increasing numbers of males coming in for counseling are from multicultural backgrounds which presents unique opportunities and challenges for them and their counselors.

5. There are important similarities and distinctions related to cultural, family, class, economic, gender backgrounds. So this is about celebrating our cultures, uniqueness/ commonalities....and about coming home to ourselves.

6. We all have privilege (ex.,food clothing shelter, healthcare, some used for positive, some not/ Blind Side, Navatar)/ biases/from growing up in culture of fear/ some ex's of RS's priv, white hetero male/able bodied, educated/biases, women should stay at home, hetero men are macho/gay men are effeminate.

7. Depending upon family and culture, messages little boys learn about _how_ to be men often include qualities like being tough, competitive, not crying or being vulnerable, always being in control, powerful, successful..self worth is based on externals/ accomplishments/ goals, material wealth/ basic human needs for comfort, safety, nurturance, respect, acceptance, connection are all too often overlooked.

8. Depending on family and culture, initiation rites of passage/traditions/rituals/mentor- ing/ role models for entering into manhood have been lost in this highly industrialized world – often resulting in the emphasis on competitive sports, gangs, overindulgence in aod..any of the miriad of distractions, gambling, internet etc., just to feel ok/adequate as a man.

9. Dark side of competition- to be #1 at all costs, no matter who you need to walk over to get there, becomes a value....no matter what, it's rarely good enough/I'm not good enough/ which often leads to great stress/anxiety/ depression/self-harm.

10. Some cultures allow the expression of emotions and feelings ex. anger/excitement, however, all too often, the emphasis is on being stoic and in control (for fear of being perceived as weak and vulnerable. It has been said that deep anger, sadness, and lack of ability/permission to cry and grieve loss is the main contributor to serious dis-eases amongst men.

11. Domination over others and the environment is seen as high value.....however we actually have little control over either.....which then becomes a real dilemma and significantly problematic.

12. There is often a stigma attached to asking for help – seen as shameful, fear of being viewed as or feeling weak/vulnerable (shame attached to fear of being overwhelmed by emotions....so deny have any...in order to maintain semblance of control and familiarity.

13. Feeling inadequate due to moving to new culture and not fitting in, language barriers, financial challenges, unemployment, not being adequate provider, history of trauma/abuse, imprisonment, not meeting social stereotypes of manliness, separation/divorce, longing for acceptance, safe touch, affection. all contribute to a sense of desperation and fear.

14. Issues like white heterosexual male supremacy/privilege are rarely if ever acknowledged, leading to confusion and self-blame for those who don't fit into that group.

15. Since men are not allowed to voice fear, even though we all live in cultures of fear- given the economy, poverty, terrorism, global warming, violence, wars...anxiety and depression related dis-ease are rampant.

Treatment/Self-Care Strategies(excerpts from R.Schiraldi WhitePrivilege Journal Article:

1. <u>Be willing to continue uncovering our own privilege and biases as we continue to work on enhancing our self-awareness so we can become more comfortable talking about diversity and privilege with peers and clients. For example, keep a white privilege journal of reminders and new learnings about our biases and privilege, as we continue to affirm and acknowledge our efforts.</u>

2. Remember that this can be hard work, that takes a lot of empathy and courage. So it's important to be gentle and compassionate with ourselves. For example, taking lots of deep breaths, and giving ourselves lots of "atta girls" and "atta boys", and breathing in comfort and words of nurturance and encouragement.

3. Look for allies. This work is too hard to do alone. Finding others who feel the same way, can be so helpful in preventing burnout and discouragement. While it might be difficult to find allies to do this work – it is essential. If there are no internal work related groups, there are usually some organizations in the

community which address privilege and multicultural concerns.

4. Believe in ourselves and our clients. We can make a difference and so can they, one little step at a time, one person at a time. Keep a journal of our efforts and encourage our clients to do the same. Graphing progress can also be useful in keeping our challenges and progress in perspective.

5. Be prepared for negative reactions to our efforts and try not to take them personally. The issue of privilege brings up a wide range of feelings in people. Journaling, mindfulness meditation and non-violent communication can be very helpful in providing self-comfort as we acknowledge our feelings and needs and other's feelings and needs. When people are feeling unsafe and threatened, they will often react negatively.

6. Let our clients know we are open to discussing these issues. For example, have pictures, books and artifacts in our offices that help make it clear of our sensitivity to multicultural issues. When appropriate, share our interest in discussing these issues.

7. Be respectful of family, name, religious, cultural traditions.....***don't assume that because we have similarities our experience and feelings are the same.

8. Ask about family/cultural messages about what boys learn about becoming men, initiation rituals, role models.

9. Making empathetic connection (some hook to get them to stay) ex. what is the fundamental pain he's struggling with, and collaborating to address the pain.

10. Managing issues of control and seeming resistance....go with it (motivational interviewing), ex. "I know you don't want to be here, we can work together to best use this time, you have the power, lock box, you have the key/ control over trauma/feelings".

11. Acknowledge how difficult it is to talk about pain/normalize physical symptoms, irritability, sleep, headaches, risky behavior, all common when feel alienated. Takes courage to be willing to learn compassion/healing...however if don't, will continue to feel less than man.

12. Be real – demystify the process, use humor, takes time to forge the relationship (perhaps small talk at first).

13. Support our clients in learning how to deal with feeling different and disconnected, for example through offering support groups that address related issues such as multi-cultural concerns, being male/teaching our young men how to be gentle with themselves and our world (Kivel, 1993), healthy relationships, and managing emotions, with approaches such as dialectical behavior therapy (Marra, 2005), mindfulness meditation (Kabat-Zinn,1990),and learning how to meet basic human needs such as acceptance, connection, empathy, through learning the art of non-violent communication (Rosenberg, 2003). Each of these approaches teach specific tools about learning self-respect and emotional management with ourselves and empathetic connection with others. Help them learn language of feelings, bodily sensations (tension etc.), emotional regulation log, practice sharing feelings. Compassion Focused Therapy/ compassionate self talk practice. Not taking away defenses until have something to replace them with, ex. NVC, needs, compassionate self-talk/actions.

14. Remind ourselves and our clients, about our internal worth, rather than looking for external

validation (G. Schiraldi, 2001). Help them learn how to celebrate their uniqueness, and of their interconnectedness to all other living things. For example use the crystal picture found in chapter four of Schiraldi's Self-esteem Workbook, to demonstrate how our essence is worthiness, however we've often been taught a belief system that focuses on materialism and external validation. Look for opportunities to encourage a radical paradigm shift to believing in self-worth, as a given/ our essence, not having to earn it, viewing accomplishments as "gravy". Have fun and be willing to consider creative approaches. As difficult as this work can be, it is very exciting, enriching and rewarding. Keep a list of new approaches, strategies, tools gained from attending trainings – especially those that help us laugh, as keeping a good sense of humor is so important in doing this work.

15. And finally, if you really want to go for it- Consider setting an intention, making a pledge, writing a commitment letter (whatever works), to address cultural competency and privilege in an ongoing way, personally and professionally, for example, discussing it with friends and

colleagues, getting more training, attending the annual White Privilege Conference, asking for support from your boss to have staff training, joining work groups which address cultural competence, and maybe even (take a deep breath) being willing to give up some of our privilege, temporarily or permanently, in whatever way feels right to us for example, eat less or periodically fasting, donate time or money to charitable and social justice causes, conserve energy or recycle. *Please remember to be gentle and kind with our precious selves.and all life, The Greatest Strength Is True Gentleness-Lakota, Mitakuye Oyasin*

White Heterosexual Male Privilege. Why every counselor should feel comfortable discussing it.

Submitted by F. Roberto Schiraldi,
EdD, LPC, LCADC

White Heterosexual Male Privilege. Why is this an important concept to explore for us counselors?

Many of our clients, especially those of color, those from different cultural or socio-economic backgrounds, LGBTQ individuals, and individuals with disabilities, feel disenfranchised, disempowered, and alienated, feeling like they simply just don't fit in. I believe that one of the primary roles as counselors should be to provide a safe haven where our clients can address these issues.

The important work of intersectionality theory can be helpful to better understand the challenges that many of our clients face. Intersectionality theory examines how there may be many factors which intersect on multiple and often simultaneous levels, thus contributing to systematic and social inequity. These factors may include biological, social and cultural categories such as gender, race, class, economic status, ability, sexual orientation, and other measures of identity (Anderson, Collins, 2003).

Fear can breed insecurity and the striving for more power, wealth, and control to give the illusion of security. Power, wealth and control create privilege, and the more some have, the less others have. Those who have power may often stereotype and perceive homogeneity because their perceptions are rarely challenged by those not in power (Fine, 1997; Keltner, 2003). It is a self-perpetuating cycle.

While there are many forms of privilege, I will here refer to the term white privilege, because I am a White male, because, (1) in this culture, at least, most power, wealth, and control still lies in the hands of White men, and (2) because it provides a clear context within which to explore healing. This is not about bashing wealthy White men, or anyone else. For if we have food, clothing and shelter, we have a certain privilege. We can each feel equal, powerful, and privileged in given moments. Similarly, we can each feel unequal, powerless, and unprivileged in given moments. For example, I can feel equal, powerful, and privileged after presenting on white privilege at a national conference and being enthusiastically received. However, I can also feel unequal, powerless, and unprivileged when my efforts to address the same topic were met with hesitancy and trepidation at the elite university I was employed by. While this is understandable, given the discomfort this topic can create, it can also feel discouraging.

While the term, "white privilege," initially may be uncomfortable to acknowledge, it can also be very useful in helping us to better understand how many of the members of our communities often feel marginalized. It is important for us to examine how white norms continue to exist, and how they may hinder people of color from feeling really welcomed in our schools, workplaces, and communities. Some very basic examples of white norms are the way people speak, dress, and act. If you don't imitate these norms, you don't feel like you fit in. As a counselor, I have heard many painful stories from clients who feel disenfranchised due to their race, gender, ethnicity, sexual orientation, disability, or socio-economic status.

Privilege can be viewed historically as a predominantly male issue, rooted deeply in insecurity, fear, and fight for survival. Ancient fear of women was coupled with seeing anyone outside the family or tribe or village as adversarial or enemies. In his book, *Fear Of Women,* Wolfgang Lederer (1968) a white, German psychiatrist, speaks of cavemen casting women out of the caves during menstruation, and when they were about to give birth. It is not hard to imagine the awe and fear experienced

Roberto Schiraldi

by the men as they witnessed the incredible mystery of women's ability to give life – the most powerful gift. That fear was compounded by the insecurity and vulnerability of having an appendage between their legs.

So it seems likely that the quest for power and control had its roots in the need to overcompensate for feelings of jealousy, vulnerability, insecurity, and fear.

Most discriminatory behavior today is very subtle (Sue, 2004) and unintentional. As someone who has attended many trainings on white privilege, I will attest to how useful that experience has been in helping me examine my own privilege, even though I had never seen myself as someone who had a great deal of privilege (Aneis, 2001), and certainly not as someone who harbored any biases or prejudices. However, when I realized that we all have certain privileges and biases, and felt safe enough to acknowledge and examine them, then I could start addressing them.

It can be helpful for us to understand that the color of our skin, (or our gender, socio-economic class, sexual orientation and being able bodied), may automatically entitle us to privilege, status, and being part of the norm. People of color often do not feel like they fit into this norm, no matter how much they try to conform. Inequity, power, and privilege can hurt us all. For if some of us feel diminished, then so are we all. And the burden of achieving and maintaining the "top" position can lead to a fragile and illusory sense of worth, as well as premature stress-related illness and heart attacks.

Cooperation and inclusion are the hallmarks of a compassionate and respectful community. Competitiveness, the pursuit of excellence at all costs, and of supremacy, power and control, are hallmarks of elitism and privilege, (and lest we forget, were the antecedents of the doctrine of Manifest Destiny, and of the resulting genocide of Native Americans, and of slavery). This is not about evoking guilt (we are not guilty for the sins of our forefathers). However, it is important that we remember and continue to learn from our history. With this understanding we will be better able to continue to help make our schools, work places, and our culture healthier environments for all of us.

Traditional Buddhist wisdom teaches "in the heart of the darkness is the light." So too, it may very well be that deep within the roots of privilege lie the essential ingredients for the healing of our world, i.e., seeing and treating all life as sacred (Marshall,2001; Mohatt, Eagle Elk, 2002), unique, worthwhile, precious, and interconnected —we are all relatives, all living things are related, as reflected in the main teachings of Lakota, Buddhist, and other great spiritual traditions. Many individuals use their privilege to make the world a better place by adopting children, contributing to social justice causes, etc. Thus, privilege isn't necessarily a bad or a good, it depends how it's used.

When we counselors are comfortable in acknowledging our own privilege, then we are much more able to make it easier for our clients who come from different backgrounds to feel welcome and safe in our presence. *(Most of this article is excerpted from a longer article by the author originally published in the White Privilege Journal / Understanding & Dismantling Privilege /**The official journal of the White Privilege Conference and the Matrix Center for the Advancement of Social Equity and Inclusion**).*

References

Anderson, M., & Collins, P.(2003), *Race, Class, Gender: An Anthology.* Michigan: Cengage Learning.

Aneis, J., & Szymanski, D.(2001) *Awareness of White Privilege Among White Counseling Trainees.* Counseling Psychologist, 29, 548-569.

Fine, M., Weiss, L., Powell, L.C., & Wong, L.M. (1997). *Off White: Readings on race, power and society.* New York: Routledge.

Keltner, D., Anderson, C., Gruenfeld, D. (2003). *Power, approach, and inhibition*. Psychological Review, 110, 265-284.

Lederer, W. (1968). *The Fear Of Women*. New York: Harcourt.

Marshall, J.M. (2001). *The Lakata Way*. New York: Penquin Putnam.

Mohatt, G., Eagle Elk, J., (2002). *The price of a gift: A Lakota Healer's Story*. Lincoln: University of Nebraska Press.

Sue, D.W., (2004). *Whiteness and ethnocentric monoculturalism: Making the "invisible" visible*. American Psychologist, 59, 761-769.

Healing From The Trauma Of Racism

Conceptualizing the experience of racism survivors through the prism of trauma survivors can be helpful in addressing multicultural counseling and racial justice work. An important element in helping our marginalized clients to heal from inter-generational and current racial trauma lies in understanding accurate history of the values that founded this country. Native Americans and slaves being viewed as savages, sub-human, property (see U.S. Constitution), is the antecedent to how marginalized groups, but especially African Americans, are still treated. So understanding and acknowledging the real history of America can be an important tool for counselors to aid in the healing of their clients from marginalized backgrounds.

As any trauma worker knows, there is no freedom, no healing, without first acknowledging the truth of the traumatic experiences that happened and continue to happen every day. Applied to race, there is only the facade of "post-racial". Trauma survivors would be crazy to accept (and perhaps only in the future, after extensive work with rage, deep grief, fear, compassion and self-care), forgive, or possibly trust a perpetrator, without first receiving sincere acknowledgment of what occurred, followed by consistently demonstrated behavior change over a long, long time. Given the continual murders, incarcerations, and other injustices and disparities, it is our responsibility as counselors to help our clients, who are racial trauma survivors, to explore these realities, if they are to have a fair chance at healing and navigating this often harsh society.

Why would a Black person trust a white counselor (or professor) who doesn't acknowledge the truth about how the value system that founded this country (and still runs it) – manifest destiny – white supremacy, white heterosexual male privilege - superiority, success, competition to be #1 at all costs no matter who or what you need to step over to get there, power, wealth, control, elitism, entitlement - the same value system that continues to keep all marginalized groups down? Many white people, of course, don't live by those values. But all too often, those in power do.

Conversely, there is much more likelihood that African American clients and clients from other marginalized groups will be drawn to counselors who are comfortable in discussing these issues. It is a wonderful benefit to the white counselor to more fully gain the respect, trust and confidence of their clients from marginalized populations. To address "cultural competency", we have to start with the question of why it's even necessary i.e., the root cause, the value system, (fear not love). If we don't address the unhealthy values, nothing changes, and the poison continues to permeate individuals and society, even with the best intentions.

On-going training, familiarity and comfort with discussing such concepts as intersectionality theory, white privilege/white supremacy, microaggressions, and broaching are essential for counselors to feel confident in their ability to provide a safe and welcoming counseling environment for their clients who come from different backgrounds. Intersectionality theory examines the many ways individuals can have privilege or lack thereof, i.e., race, class, gender, sexual orientation, disabilities, with many experiencing more than one simultaneously, and the resulting consequences. White privilege and white supremacy looks at power differences based on skin color - that can benefit some and hinder others. Microagressions are usually unconscious and unintended hurtful treatment of others who are different. And broaching explores the characteristics, attitudes and behaviors involved in helping us feel more comfortable in addressing racial and other differences with our colleagues, and our clients.

It is no coincidence that when it comes to proposing the need for increased multicultural counseling training, about the aforementioned topics, the discussion is often divides clearly along racial lines. White folks are often afraid and defensive when it comes to acknowledging our country's painful history and our own privilege. One concern often voiced is, "Where does it stop?", "Will we continually be forced to bring up past racial injustice?", Can't we just move beyond this?" To me, the reply is, "As long as it takes". No other group is close to being murdered and incarcerated at the rate of African Americans, other than Native Americans. This will not change until we first acknowledge our history and commit ourselves to continual learning, self-exploration, and justice.

A related point......Many years ago when I worked at Temple University, in preparation for possibly being forced to use the DSM, the question we wrestled with was, "are there really disorders?" (a paternalistic, white heterosexual male privilege label), or is it, more accurately, a "disordered society" to which we humans are merely reacting / adjustment reactions?). This is similar to the concept of the "Addictive Society" which Anne Wilson Shaef talked about in her seminal book, in which addicts are described as the "scapegoats" for a dysfunctional society.

Most African Americans, and other people of color, know intuitively about the aforementioned disparities of treatment and history. It's in their DNA, passed on from generations. White folks have to be taught it....since, because of our privilege, we don't have to be aware of it.

This is such a vital issue for us as healers and as advocates for our clients. It is not about guilt or blame. We have all been hurt. We have all hurt others. We cannot truly understand another unless we have walked in their shoes. And we counselors, especially white counselors, have rarely had enough training and experience in addressing these issues. This is difficult, often messy work, which requires courage, compassion, integrity and perseverance. We will not do it perfectly. We can however, do our best to continue to uncover our own unconscious biases and privilege, and keep learning and growing from our mistakes.

This is also about acknowledging and taking responsibility to work for change. We need to be change advocates. Again, anyone who has been traumatized needs to acknowledge what happened for healing to begin. Denial will only keep us stuck. Having worked with individuals with addictions, sexual assault/trauma survivors, victims of homophobia, sexism, ageism, ableism and racism my whole career, it is clear to me, that we healers and educators need lots more training in how to best support ourselves and our clients to effectively address these issues. This is not just one course....this needs to be a life-long commitment to self-exploration and learning.

Remembering that the above is true (not minimizing or denying), that "All Life Is Sacred, that We Are All Related, and We Are All One!". Let the healing begin.

Dr. Roberto Schiraldi
February 2016

Mental health and wealthy white hetero male supremacy culture....the Dilemma

Mental health can be viewed as a result of experiencing a balanced life...emotionally, mentally, spiritually, physically, socially.....and a belief in one's self-worth. Few of us have been raised by perfect parents. So it is up to each of us to choose a belief in and acceptance of our core worth. If our worth depends on external circumstances or influences, such as our accomplishments, job, material wealth, and approval of others, our sense of self-worth will be transitory at best. It is up to us to choose, to decide that our essence is whole and worthwhile...and that all other aspects like feelings, ailments, highs and lows, are just part of life, and don't really affect our true self-worth.

While there are many contributing factors to mental illness, I believe that one huge cause has rarely been touched on....the culture of wealthy white heterosexual male supremacy. This cultural value system of wealthy white hetero male supremacy which most of us have been raised in, is at this very moment in history being severely tested, especially given the combination of the nationwide protests of continual murders of Black men, and the life threatening corona virus. I don't believe there is any coincidence that these two major life-altering events are simultaneously occurring. I believe that both of these events are happening at this exact moment in time, to hopefully awaken our sense of outrage at the life threatening value system of wealthy white heterosexual male supremacy, which is the root cause of most, if not all of the dysfunctionality and pain that plagues our society. This system is a major cause of mental disease, disorders...because we are dwelling in a disordered culture of fear, where our very humanity, and sense of self-worth is never good enough. We, (especially we men), have been taught that a sense of our okay'ness depends on so many things outside of our control. This leads to incredible stress related illness and mistrust of ourselves and each other...especially of other men of color, who have been perceived as a huge threat since the beginning of this country. This is because, while there were some good "intentions", the country was never founded on true equality and justice for all.... only for the few wealthy white heterosexual men (the Constitution excluded Native People and Women, and claimed African American males as 3/5ths of a person, while the Declaration of Independence declared Native People as "savages". Mental health largely depends

Roberto Schiraldi

on living with impeccable integrity, compassion and humility for ourselves and all others. These qualities have never been more questioned that at this present moment.

So let us explore what the words ....wealthy...white.... heterosexual....male.....supremacy imply...so we can better understand the impact on our lives.

wealthy white hetero male supremacy terms defined:

wealthy – land owning, material wealth, has been a key value for power since the beginning of this country, and a symbol of success, achievement, **worth,** prestigious.

white – white is right, at least in this culture, is key, given that the white supremacy cultural system of racism was started and still run by predominantly white males, white seen as good, Black and other colors not as good, or even bad, evil, certainly at least, less than, not as smart.

hetero – next key ingredient.....almost synonymous with masculinity, fear of being seen as weak/gay/ effeminate/vulnerable, don't share feelings, rational, macho --Fear of Women, penis envy, women secondary.

male is the key ingredient...has been since the beginning of time....male cultural values...competition to be #1

at all costs, power, material wealth, control, success, rational/unemotional, aggressive,

supremacy – to be in charge, at the top, the most important, to have all the power, superior/supreme, #1, to aspire to, entitled, elite, rulers of the land, animals, all others...(almost god like).....

......while most self-secure men would not claim the above as their core values....one cannot deny that these were the core values and still are in terms of who has the power in this country.

The above warrants a lot more examination.....because if the roots are still poisoned, so will the efforts towards growth be poisoned. I hope that at least some of this essay touches you and supports you in understanding how peeling away the layers of our white heterosexual male supremacy culture will begin to free us to work towards healthier mental health. Balanced emotional, mental, physical, spiritual, social health demands courageous truth telling and compassionate action for us to feel secure inside, and to make things right.

I offer these words below for comfort and encouragement for each of us......

Breathing in, breathing out...

I am whole and worthy, exactly the way I am

I serve all others with my whole heart and my whole spirit.

May it be so.

Broaching

Addressing and/or responding to racially offensive comments, attitudes and behaviors.

Our comfort or discomfort with broaching issues of race, ethnicity, culture, sexual orientation, white privilege/white supremacy etc., can be crucial in building trust with clients, and connecting with others.

Broaching Characteristics, Attitudes and Behaviors

1. (Integrated /Congruent) /Characteristics-
Broaching is regarded as an important aspect of life.

Attitude Toward Broaching-
Committed towards broaching and towards eradicating all forms of oppression

Broaching behavior-
Broaching represents a lifestyle orientation, continues to self examine and encourages others.

2. (Incongruent)/Characteristics-
Openness to but lacks accompanying skills and confidence, concerned about reactions of others

Attitude Towards Broaching-
Recognizes the importance but hesitant due to discomfort

Broaching Behavior-
Occasionally, but limited strategies, feels mechanical and superficial

3. (Avoidant)/Characteristics-
Ignores, minimizes and maintains race neutral perspective

Attitude Towards Broaching-
Oblivion, resistance, defensiveness, feels it's unnecessary

Broaching Behavior-
Refusal to broach

So the continuum looks like this:

Avoidant   Incongruent   Integrated/Congruent

The idea is to ask ourselves where do we fit. This is not about guilt or self-criticism, or right or wrong. It's about understanding, with compassion, why we are where we are. And if we would like to change, coming up with well-thought out strategies to practice changing. It is usually a fluid continuum. Most of us move back and forth depending upon how we're feeling, our tiredness, frustration, self-care, etc.

None of us is perfect. This is messy work. Please remember when considering broaching or addressing someone, to always do our best to hold ourselves in a place of love, and acceptance, and compassion, and to do our best to hold the other in a place of love, acceptance and compassion.....and most of all...RESPECT. If we're feeling ungrounded and angry, it will likely not result in mutually positive outcome. Kindness, consideration, understanding go a long way to bridging/connecting across the differences. Please be kind with yourself. If we feel respected and understood we are much more likely to be receptive to the other. **(Based on work of Day-Vines et al., Journal of Counseling and Devlopment, Fall 2007)**

To Broach (for a counselor)

So you want to be a counselor
and multicultural too?......
no easy task
here in our red,, white and blue.

To broach
or not to broach, that is the question
Specially when a racist slur
gives us indigestion.

We can change the subject
or pretend we didn't hear her
but then how do we
look ourselves in the mirror?

Implicit bias,
or micro-agression,
to be addressed,
in a counseling session?
Hmmmm......

First we look inside
and check how we're feelin
what we need to feel ok

before we start dealin.

Then we speak our truth
with <u>love</u>...we can't go wrong
compassionate <u>hearts</u>
gentle, brave, and strong.

Perhaps, asking for help
in understanding,
rather than <u>attacking,</u>
or critically demanding.

This isn't easy work
can be messy, filled with pain.
Yet when we do our parts
there's so much to gain.

We connect to ourselves
we connect to each other.
Everyone our sister
Everyone our brother.

September 2019

The Ethics of Broaching

(From Love Poems on white supremacy)

Fearlessly speaking our truth....

....with love.

When I hear
or see
or feel

comments
expressions
behaviors
that wound
that hurt
that cut....deep

threatening peoples' safety
and sense of well-being
sense of dignity
and sense of worth....

This broaching
not for the meek of heart.
Takes courage

and compassion
and commitment
to step up
and take a stand..
for fairness and equity
and justice.....
...and kindness.

...to be bold
in owning
and holding ourselves
accountable
responsible.....
welcoming and embracing
every opportunity...

for making the world
a better place
for us **all.**

Not just
wealthy, white, hetero males...

for Native folks
Black folks, Latino folks, Asian folks
Gay, straight, Trans
Folks with disabilities, able bodied

Women, men
children, animals, trees....
...ALL Life.

If not here....where?
If not now....when?
If not us counselors....who?

September 2019

Holding Space For Transformation and Communicating Non-Violently

These are two of the most important racial justice tools for addressing micro and macroagressions, or any type of racial bullying. They were taught to me by two of my most precious teachers, Dr. Amanda Aminata Kemp, and Eliane Gerin.

Below I have summarized what I feel to be the heart of both approaches. I have found these processes to be soooo helpful....for my sanity, for my health, for my growth. Of course, they take lots and lots of practice. Best to only engage when feeling full of love and wisdom. These are the steps:

1. Breathe deeply.....so deeply...into the heart of mother earth....feeling grounded, feet solidly planted, balanced, connected to the loving power, wisdom, compassion of the earth mother and the universe.

2. Continuing to breathe, checking in with my wise self, am I balanced, solid, clear, feeling my compassionate self, (if not, maybe best to hold off). If feeling solid, I breathe in and say to myself, "I am unconditional love, I am

unconditional acceptance, and then, "I offer unconditional love and unconditional acceptance to the other". Feeling seeing you both in that space of unconditional love and unconditional acceptance.

3. With genuine interest and curiosity for the other, ask them if they would be willing to share with you what they were feeling, meaning, intending, and why they said or did whatever it was. This should only be done in a one to one, not in front of others. Asking them if they would be willing to help you understand. And then repeat what you heard to be sure you got it right. If this is done with compassion and kindness, it can work. However, when done in a confrontational way.....fuhgetaboudit.

If you have more time to consider before addressing the individual:

Objectively consider what happened...the facts, words, actions, if possible without judgment (I know that's a big ask).
Check in with what your feelings, i.e., anger, fear, sadness

Ask yourself what you are needing i.e., safety, respect, consideration etc.

Speak to yourself in a way that meets the need, i.e., "I respect you, I appreciate you, I know that really hurt or made you angry.

If you still feel motivated to speak with the other, and *only if* you trust the person, and/or the person seems open to meeting you in a mutual heart space, you might ask them if they'd be open to discussing what just happened, then if they are, take some guesses by asking them what you think they might have felt and needed and wanted, ie., when you said that, were you feeling angry, because you were needing respect?, Is there some way I can support you with this?

I've found that when I take a genuine interest in someone, they often respond in a positive way. However, it sure ain't easy, especially when emotions get charged. So often it's best to initially take a break and do the self work, and then decide if it's still a good idea to proceed with the other.

Afterwards, gently acknowledge self, check in with needs, nourish self, give prayer of gratitude.

Calling Out / Calling In

Outside the gates of Princeton University, one of my favorite warrior woman allies Linda R. and I were doing a Saturday, two person, "Stand For Racial Justice" demonstration. She usually does it alone. I just wanted to support her. We proudly held our "Stand For Racial Justice" signs. I had my "Black Lives Matter" t-shirt on, and my hat with the medicine wheel symbol from the Rosebud Reservation where I went for many years to learn Native healing traditions.

Passers-by were mostly civil, or they just smiled and shook their heads as if to say, "why are they doing this?" Some stopped by to say thank you, and some gave us thumbs up or peace signs. All in all, seemed like a pretty good day.

And then.

A car drove by with a bunch of folks calling out, "All lives matter, you racists", and I think, some expletive deletives. I gave them the peace sign. At least they didn't throw anything at us.

Then a little while later another car drives by, and the driver yells out the exact same thing, "All lives matter, you racists". I again gave him the peace sign. He then does a u-turn and pulls over in front of us. I said to myself, oh boy, here we go. He gets out of the car, and I walk over to him.

And then a miracle happens.

I am sure that Great Spirit came down and infused me with clarity, calm, strength, and compassion. In the past, it wouldn't have been pretty. I said to the guy...."You know, you're right....all lives do matter.....and we've all been screwed by the wealthy one percenters, and pitted against each other". He paused a second, and then said,,,,,"You're right!". He told me he was an retired officer in the Marine Corps. I told him I was a Vietnam era vet, who worked in an intensive care psychiatric unit an army hospital with the traumatized vets who came home from Vietnam.

We ended up talking a little more, and he ends up giving me his card and telling me he gives tours of the local battlefields around Princeton. We ended up hugging each other. Who'da thunk it?

I know it was the Great Spirit's way of reminding me, that "calling-in", with genuine compassion, quietly, one to one, with respect, and understanding, and a desire to take a genuine interest in and connect with the other, is the way to go. Not "calling out" with anger, confrontation and ego driven competition to prove the other wrong, especially done in front of others.

I've been able to do that a number of times. I've

also not been so successful, on a lot of other occasions, when I let my anger, frustration, rage, and deep sense of injustice run the show.

This sure ain't easy. That's puttin it mildly. I do know one thing for sure. Giving myself lots and lots of love and compassion, gentleness, kindness, understanding and encouragement it what I need to keep doing this work. I also need the support of my loving, supportive racial justice allies. I also need to follow the loving advise from some of my amazing racial justice mentors who remind me of the necessity to pace myself, take breaks, rest and care for myself regularly..,,,, So......I''m gonna listen to them right now..... and breathe.... and smile.....and sign off. Thanks for listening.

Double Jeopardy!

Implications of Healing From Trauma For Native, African American and Other Veterans Of Color

Many Veterans of Color are very proud of their military service. And they certainly deserve to be. However, for many, sharing stories and feelings about the traumatic effects of military service on themselves and other veterans of color can be a very challenging problem. The following statement, and article which follows, summarize some of the sentiments I have heard from fellow veterans of color since serving in the military back in 1969 - "I'm supposed to feel proud of my service, and I am. However, I am part of a war machine that massacred and enslaved my ancestors, and continues to enforce unjust policies here and around the world, often against other poor people of color".

This can be a painful, and morally conflicting dilemma.

I am a white male Vietnam Era veteran. So where do I get off writing about trauma for veterans of color? As a white male veteran, I feel it is my responsibility to speak on this topic, since it is still predominantly white

Roberto Schiraldi

males who hold the power in our government and in the military. And since the beginning of our country to the present, it is primarily us white males who have perpetrated the violence against people of color, women, children, animals, the environment.

After my infantry training, and combat medic training, I was trained to be a neuro-psychiatric specialist, serving in an intensive care psychiatric unite of an army hospital. While there I was honored to work with and learn from many veterans of color, and experienced first hand the often very excruciating difficulties they had to deal with, and are still having to deal with.

During most of my career as a trauma therapist and racial justice advocate, I have been taught by many of my sister and brother veterans of color about the unique challenges facing them and that all too often go unspoken, due to rage, guilt, shame, fear. So it my hope to shed some additional light on how necessary it is for us to promote preventative training about these issues and to ensure improved services to our veterans of color as a step in healing the wounds.

Post-traumatic stress disorder, PTSD, was not a term we used back in 1969. As the Vietnam "conflict" was winding down, many combat veterans were hospitalized in intensive care psychiatric units as a result of the horrific atrocities they experienced.

Reflecting back now on some of the veterans of color I worked with on the wards and alcohol and other drug rehab wards, I am struck by the almost impossible situation they found themselves in. They were not treated like full-fledged citizens, yet expected to put their lives on the line, and go kill other people of color who they had no grudge with.

This brings to mind Muhammad Ali – brave enough to make a stand, yet having to sacrifice the best years of his career.

Many of our veterans in Vietnam were ordered to commit unthinkable acts against innocent men, women and children, or face being shot themselves, court-martialed and long term imprisonment for disobeying orders. Then they return home from the trauma of war, to their country, and were not welcomed as heroes, but were met with protests and criticism. And veterans of color were thrust back into a country caught in the middle of heightened awareness of painful civil rights injustices, compounded by intergenerational racial trauma, which is only now beginning to get the attention it deserves. They were and still are, often faced with "red-lining" practices to prevent buying homes in certain neighborhoods, as well as many other discriminatory practices like when applying for jobs and bank loans, and racial profiling.

Roberto Schiraldi

I was drafted while serving as a Teacher Corps Intern, as part of the government's anti-poverty programs. Along with some Vista volunteers we would apply to rent or buy from landlords or real estate agents who had turned down African American Veterans. Attorneys would then step in to help enforce fair housing practices.

Many Native American veterans experienced shame for feeling like they betrayed their people by serving in the military. Their ancestors had been raped and massacred by U.S. soldiers, and survivors forced to travel to desolate reservations where poverty is rampant to this day. Alcoholism, other drug addiction, extreme domestic violence and abuse, suicide, many physical diseases and ailments, can be directly linked to the injustices which have never been rectified

I worked with a veteran on the psych ward who had been a member of the Black Panthers when he was drafted. As with many of us, being faced with jail or having to leave the country, he chose to serve. Being torn inside about the killing he participated in while in Vietnam, as a Black man / Black Panther, led him to be suicidal/homicidal and eventually to the psych. ward. Being faced with returning to his city feeling unwelcome, even a traitor to his people, was untenable to him. This was just one of many similar stories of the painful dilemmas facing African American and other veterans of color. It is not only the aforementioned injustices, but the often unspoken guilt and shame which is responsible for many suicides, alcoholism, other drug addiction, domestic violence and abuse and many physical diseases and ailments.

A few years back I attended a powerful meeting in NYC of a group called Intersections which hosted small group discussions to address these stories to heal the guilt and shame.

War is hell for all soldiers. However, it is certainly a lot clearer to me now, that as a white heterosexual male, I didn't have to deal with the same level of traumatic stress that my Native, Black, Latino, and other veterans of color, women and gay sister and brother veterans did and still do. This includes harassing, oppressive treatment by fellow soldiers and those in charge.

It is way past time that we address the impact that military service can have on the mental, emotional and physical health of our veterans of color. Training for government, military leaders, mental health and other health care professionals is essential about how to best prevent and reduce levels of trauma, and how to acknowledge and tend to their treatment needs.

Thank you.

Roberto Schiraldi

("In the Second World War over a million African-Americans fought for freedom and democracy - in an army, that was strictly segregated by race. These African-American GIs fought to liberate Germany from Nazi rule, where racism had reached a dimension that was unfathomable. Narrated by Academy-Award winner Cuba Gooding, Jr. and featuring interviews with former Secretary of State General Colin Powell and Congressman John Lewis, this is the remarkable story of how World War II and its aftermath played a huge role in the Civil Rights Movement. It's a story told through the powerful recollections of veterans like Charles Evers, brother of slain Civil Rights icon Medgar Evers or Tuskegee ace pilot Roscoe Brown. **From the beginning, black soldiers felt the absurdity of being asked to fight for freedom while being denied it in their own army.**"

(From the highly recommended documentary "Breath of Freedom", available on internet / Vimeo / Broadway on Demand, December 2014.))

*(The following is an outline for a core curriculum course that has been proposed in seeking increased training in multicultural counseling for all counselors, as well as for improvement in public school racial literacy education.)

Outline for Core Curriculum Course

I. <u>Accurate History</u>. **Acknowledging key components of US history ("Racial Literacy"), provides a context and implications for addressing current individual and societal problems.** It is incredibly challenging to heal intergenerational racial trauma wounds of the past and present without first acknowledging some of the painful historical truths that were part of the founding of our country and are likely continuing to contribute to our current racial problems. Having a "common understanding" of our accurate history is essential for sustainable healing.

A. <u>Genocide of Native Americans</u>

Mass killing of Native Americans
Doctrine of Discovery, God's Anointed Ones, Manifest Destiny, as the ideology to justify Europeans' economic advancement **at all costs**

Seneca form of tribal government used as model for
democracy
Removal Act of 1830
Intentional exposure to smallpox
Forcing children to separate from their families and
communities by sending them to boarding schools
and forced to assimilate
Slaughter of buffalo, starvation, and social and cultural
disintegration of many Plains tribes.
Economic disintegration of many Plains tribes due to
many treaties violated by US government.
Present situation: Still mostly confined to reservations,
poverty, poor education, and minimal job
opportunities.
Contributions by Native Americans to American culture
Understanding   and   acknowledging   resulting
intergenerational trauma is necessary for healing and
trust building to begin. (Truth and Reconciliation
Commission of Canada, South African Truth and
Reconciliation Commission as examples)
There are many Native Americans in NJ, for example the
Nanticoke Lenni-Lenape. Many African Americans
have Native American ancestry, many multiracial
people have Native American ancestry. Territorial
acknowledgment, created in consultation with
Indigenous people, is one way to demonstrate respect

for their history and culture when hosting training programs and organizational meetings.

Bibliography: 1. NJ Dept. Of Education. Amistad Commission http://njamistadcurriculum.org 2. Zinn Education Project http://zinnedproject.org 3. *An Indigenous People's History of the United States (Revisioning American History)* by Roxanne Dunbar Ortiz (2014) 4. Truth and Reconciliation Commission of Canada http://www.trc.ca/websites/trcinstitution/index.php?p=3 5. *"Race: The Power of an Illusion"*, Three-part educational documentary on PBS, by California Newsreel, www.youtube.com/watch?v=Y8MS6zubIaQ. 6. *Decolonization Is Not A Metaphor,* Tuck, E., & Yang, K.W., Decolonization: Indigeneity, Education & Society, Vol. 1, No. 1, 2012, pp. 1-40.

B. Enslaved Africans Viewed as Property, Not as People, and the Legacy of Slavery

Africans intentionally chosen to be kidnapped because they were strong, smart, and master farmers

Major difference between Africans, the only group forced to come here, and all other immigrant groups that came to America by choice.

Original U.S. Constitution was written for land owning, white males

Atrocities of slavery: forced labor, torture, murder, rape, body mutilation, breakdown of family and culture.

Identifying the U.S. Presidents who owned slaves.

Civil War / real reasons for Civil War, economic/ freeing the slaves (slave labor undergirded the U.S economy.). As slaves were freed, the Ku Klux Klan and other hate groups grew in number to "protect their rights". Thus, the original manifest destiny doctrine, combined with fear of the "angry Black man" can be viewed as key components to developing implicit or unconscious bias towards African Americans as well as many other groups (such as Asians, Latinos, other immigrant groups, LGBTs, women, people with disabilities), which may be perceived as a threat to white supremacy. An effective colonization strategy used to control the masses is by pitting them against each other.

Policing system started, with bounty hunters to retrieve run away, enslaved Africans. This has clearly contributed to implicit biases within the system, seeing Black men as threatening/ fear of "angry" Black men "raping our women" etc., often leading to extreme violence against Black men, and grossly inflated incarceration of generations of Black mothers' sons and Black children's' fathers.

Post-emancipation and Reconstruction sharecropping virtually re-establishing the plantation system and Jim Crow laws (loitering, etc.) resulting in chain gangs (penal slavery).

Voting rights /still an issue for people in their communities and for those who get out of jail.

Mass incarceration and killing of young Black men.

Contributions by African Americans to American culture, regularly misappropriated by other cultures in power. Acknowledging and celebrating resiliency and joy of the resistance experience of family and social traditions of African Americans and other marginalized groups, and their huge impact on the arts, music, dance, poetry, fashion, cuisine, language arts, religion/spirituality, athletics, education, science, medicine, science, industry, business, government, etc.

Understanding and acknowledging resulting intergenerational trauma derived from this status of oppression, which is necessary for healing and trust building to begin. (Truth and Reconciliation Commission of Canada, South African Truth and Reconciliation Commission as examples).

*Understanding how the above two sections contributed to oppressive treatment of and minimizing contributions by Asian, Latinx and other people of color, and other groups to American culture i.e., manifest destiny and the U.S. Constitution for land owning white males, everyone else excluded.

Bibliography: 1. NJ Dept. Of Education. Amistad Commission http://njamistadcurriculum.org 2. Zinn Education Project http://zinnedproject.org. 3. *Slavery by Another Name: The Re-Enslavement of Black Americans from the Civil War to World War II* by Douglas Blackmon. (2009) 4. *The New Jim Crow: Mass Incarceration in the Age of Colorblindness* by Michelle Alexander (2010) 5. Hoover, Jania, *"Don't Teach Black History Without Joy"*, Education Week, February 2, 2021,

II. *Skills. Obtaining the knowledge and skills to comfortably discuss and address White Supremacy Culture, White Privilege, Intersectionality Theory, Implicit Bias, Racial Microaggressions, Broaching, Non-violent communication, and Healing From Racial Trauma, are essential ingredients for addressing racial problems.

A. White Supremacy Culture

1. <u>Understanding white supremacy culture and white supremacy cultural values</u> and how they contributed to above sections A and B). **System of power, wealth and control that founded this country and still runs it.... a hierarchy of human value, orchestrated by predominantly wealthy / land owning white heterosexual males, where inferiority and superiority are based primarily on race** …. a system which cleverly manipulates and pits all races, ethnicities, women, poor and middle-class white men, and all other groups, against the other, each competing for an equitable piece of the pie.

2. **Characteristics* and values of white supremacy culture – (Stemming from principles of "God's Anointed Ones, Doctrine of Discovery, Manifest Destiny)...leading to elitism, entitlement, superiority, hyper masculinity, competition to be #1 at all costs, no matter who you need to walk over to get there, success, power, wealth, especially material wealth, "perfectionism, sense of urgency, metered goals (often leading to "It's never quite good enough"/ "I'm never quite good enough",**

Roberto Schiraldi

multitasking, worship of the written word (if it's not in a memo, it doesn't exist), there's only one right way, "quantity over quality, defensiveness, paternalism, those in power make decisions for the group, either/or thinking, good/bad, right/ wrong, us against them, power hoarding, little if any value around sharing power, fear of open conflict, individualism rather than working as team, progress is bigger, more, objectivity, belief that there is such a thing as being objective and "neutral", scapegoating those who cause discomfort*

3.   ***** **Unhealthy/"Toxic" Masculinity** (which hurts us all) / Intersection of sexism and racism, patriarchy, capitalism, and the importance of a feminist/racial equity perspective for counseling. (Books by Jackson Katz, i.e., "Man Enough", "Leading Men", "The Macho Paradox", National Organization for Men Against Sexism). *This may be the most important factor, which significantly contributes to, and underlies all the other factors of racism. The unhealthy wealthy white hetero male supremacy cultural values which founded this country and still run it...have never been adequately acknowledged or examined...i.e., wealthy*

white heteromaledomination/patriarchy, power, wealth, control, success, elitism, entitlement, competition to be #1 at all costs, no matter who we need to walk over, and on an on. Until the wealthy, white hetero male supremacy power elite take responsibility for the values which run things, and commit to making it right....we will keep running around in circles, putting temporary band-aids on the problems. This includes the mental health and social service systems, which diagnose "problems", in order to keep the power structures in place, rather than insist on effectively treating the root causes of the problems in the first place.

4.   ** <u>**Dwelling in a culture of fear**</u>. The aforementioned unhealthy masculinity leads to dwelling in a culture of fear, where there are so many threats to "safety" and "security"....i.e., terrorism, war, climate change and environmental disasters, stress related dis-ease / pandemics, civil unrest/violence, economic volatility and on and on. 'The Fear Of Women', by Austrian Psychiatrist Wolfgang Lederer, examines how men, down through the ages have both loved and feared women (given women's incredible

power to give birth, and their connection to the mother earth..ie. burning witches etc). **Fear** of being **vulnerable,** losing "control", of not being good enough, can lead to being macho, as a cover-up., see presidential debates like two school boys posturing in the school yard....what a terrible, terrible example for our young boys. It begs the question, is fear of being gay (I.e, two men actually being vulnerable, tender and caring with each other), a core root of so many of our problems? *(Please see the amazing video 'The Wisdom of Trauma', by Dr. Gabor Mate, which explores the greatest trauma of being alienated from ourselves, and the important work of Brene Brown on being vulnerable, including her Ted Talk, 'Power of Vulnerability', and her audio CD, 'Teachings on Authenticity, Connection and Courage')*. This fear of being vulnerable, and the loving courage it takes to be so, may well hold the key to healing for us all, (Schiraldi, R., 'A White Man on the REZ, "Higher" Education in a Culture of Fear", Princeton Comment.com, April 29, 2013

5. ******Antidotes* to white supremacy cultural values / Creating a culture of Healthy Values**-Choosing to teach and model and live by agreed

upon values which **serve All** Life - Starting with our relationship with ourselves and all others, in all of our institutions... families, schools, (K-Post Grad as core mission), churches, health care/ MH, government, business and industry, law enforcement, military, prisons, and on and one, asking for commitment to core values in all life. **Teaching the core value of All Life is Sacred. Sacred, meaning...highly valued, worthwhile, important, precious, cherished, worthy of love, dignity, respect, awe and wonder. I am no better no worse than that insect, that plant, that tree, that animal, that child, that woman, that man. All Life is Sacred. Teaching about Love* as our most important value - including such essential ingredients as impeccable integrity, courage, humility, vulnerability, commitment, responsibility, cooperation, sharing, generosity, kindness, consideration, nurturance, support, encouragement, dependability, gentleness, strength, service, respect, accountability, equity, fairness. (see bell hooks,'All About Love'***).** Develop a culture of appreciation, i.e., especially in work places** - by establishing "realistic work plans/time frames, set goals of diversity and inclusion, understanding the link between

Roberto Schiraldi

defensiveness and fear of losing power, losing face, losing privilege etc., including process or quality goals in planning, to get off the agenda to hear others', concerns, learn how others communicate, come up with other ways to share information, accept there are many ways to do something and be willing to learn about other's different cultural ways of doing things, include people who are affected by decisions in the decision making process, push to come up with more than two alternatives take breaks, breathe, avoid making decisions under extreme pressure, include sharing power in your mission statement, make sure there is understanding that a good leader develops the power and skills of others, and that change is inevitable, revisit how conflict is handled, and see how it might be handled differently, create culture of group solving as value statement, create 7th generation thinking, how actions will affect seven generations from now, be open to understanding different world views, deepen understanding of racism and oppression and see how personal experience fits into the larger picture", (** "white supremacy culture", Changework, Dismantling Racism Workshop, Tema Okun).

Bibliography. Ruiz, D. M., 'The Four Agreements', Howe, M. and Howe, L. 'Values Clarification, *hooks, b., 'All About Love', Human Development Program, Charles, M, *We the People* (U-Tube Video), Wilson-Shaef, A. 'When Society Becomes The Addict', Hillman, J., Ventura, M., 'We've Had A Hundred Years of Psychotherapy and the Worlds Getting Worse', Schiraldi, G., 'Self-Esteem Workbook', Schiraldi, G., 'Complete Guide for Resiliency', Schiraldi, R. *white man on the REZ"* (Journal Article), Schiraldi, R., 'Healing Love Poems for white supremacy culture: *Living our Values'*, Schiraldi, R. 'Unexpurgated* Racial Justice Poetry with Healing Meditations'.

6. White supremacy cultural values create racism, sexism, homophobia, xenophobia, classism and all the other issues which divide and **instill mistrust** among the groups, all for the control of the few wealthy white men in power. For example, this **fear** and **mistrust** is an especially effective way of influencing working-class decision-making regarding union activities and voting.

Bibliography. Lorde, A., 'The Master's Tools Will Never Dismantle The Master's House', Penguin Random House, 2017.

7. The ongoing **mistrust** can create even more animosity during challenging times, i.e., after 911 Arab and Muslim people were often targeted, and many wore American flags to avoid attacks and being accused of being foreigners or unpatriotic. **"It is not our differences that divide us. It is our inability to recognize, accept, and celebrate those differences."– Audre Lorde. The popular notions of "melting pot", and "assimilation" which seem so attractive on one hand, can also be viewed as effective tools to lessen unique ties to cultural traditions, thus making it easier to control and manipulate.**

8. U.S. Constitution excluding Women, Native men and counting Black men as 3/5th human (to control voting power). See 'We The People', Ted Talks by Mark Charles, Navaho.

9. "We cannot change what we don't acknowledge." - James Baldwin. "When we lack a common understanding of our history, it is much more difficult to come together." - Mark Charles

10. It is curious how a country founded upon revolutionary spirit, quickly adopts a strong "nationalistic fervor", and accuses protesters of being un-American, often leading to violent

confrontations ire., Black Lives Matter and Charlottesville. **"Revolution is not a one-time event. It is becoming always vigilant for the smallest opportunity to make a genuine change in established, outgrown responses; for instance, it is learning to address each other's difference with respect. "Audre Lorde**

11. <u>Considering the implications of racial breakdown of people who control our institutions, the vast majority being white hetero males.</u> **White supremacy cultural values lead to systemic racism,** which permeates all our institutions- government, education, religion, corporations, banks, police, military, sports, health care, and <u>mental health</u>. **"The master's tools will never dismantle the master's house. They may allow us to temporarily beat him at his own game, but they will never enable us to bring about genuine change." – Audre Lorde**

12. <u>**Four hundred plus years in a white supremacy culture has yielded some improvements**</u>. **Yet racism and inequity still flourish because we haven't gotten to <u>the root cause</u>. The root cause is that "<u>All Life</u>, is not and never has been, seen as sacred, valuable, worthwhile. If it were, we wouldn't have the need for a curriculum**

about white supremacy culture. Yet hope burns eternal. And the "struggle" goes on. "If there is no struggle, there is no progress. Those who profess to favor freedom, and yet depreciate agitation, are men who want crops without plowing up the ground. They want rain without thunder and lightning. They want the ocean without the awful roar of its many waters. This struggle may be a moral one; or it may be a physical one; or it may be both moral and physical; but it must be a struggle. Power concedes nothing without a demand. It never did and it never will." — Frederick Douglass, Frederick Douglass: Selected Speeches and Writings

13. A Truth and Conciliation Process (conciliation rather than re-conciliation, which implies that there once was harmony), like those in Africa, Australia, Canada, and some related efforts in this country, have proven to be helpful in at least beginning the process of healing deeply embedded wounds. The process entails acknowledgment of injustices and atrocities, sincere, heartfelt amends, and commitment to sustainable change, vetted by those who have been oppressed and traumatized, often

inter-generationally. Of course, trust takes time to build, and then, only, if the ones in power keep to their word.

14. Impact on mental health issues with people of color and white people, from living in white supremacy culture. Mental health can be viewed as the result of a balance of mental, emotional, physical, spiritual, social aspects of our lives. Racism and it's skewed values are traumatic, the antithesis of good mental health, and extremely hurtful to our mental, emotional, physical, spiritual, and social health. The intersection of corona virus and nationwide protests against racism can be viewed as the simultaneous result of a systemic history of dis-ease disorders... because we are all dwelling in a disordered culture of fear, where our very humanity and sense of self-worth depends on so many things outside of our control. This leads to incredible stress related illness and mistrust of ourselves and each other, especially those who we perceive as "different", and a threat.

Bibliography. 1. Bryant-Davis, T. (2007). *Healing requires recognition: The case for race-based traumatic stress.* The Counseling Psychologist,35,135-142., 2.

Hemmings, C. Evans, A. *Identifying and Treating Race Based Trauma in Counseling*(2018), Journal of Multicultural Counseling and Development, Vol 46. Issue 1 20-39IV, 3. Telusma, B., *Do We All Have PTSD? Mental Health in an age of racial terror.* Grio, March 27, 2018.

15. Implications of white supremacy culture on counseling profession i.e., many counselors over diagnose clients of color, and miss racial trauma diagnosis. It is essential that counselors understand how white supremacy culture leads to racial trauma and resulting stress related dis-eases which affect us all. And the concept of "disorder", might well be replaced with adjustment reaction to a dis-ordered society (a la Anne Wilson Schaef's seminal book *"When Society Becomes an Addict."*

16. **Ethical implications of lack of necessary anti-racism training for all counselors**. A study published in the Journal of Multicultural Counseling and Development investigated "**Are counselors really addressing the issue of race-based trauma?**" It found that the *majority of counselors in the United States are **not prepared to identify and treat***

race-based trauma, which often results from racial harassment, discrimination, violence, or experiencing institutional Racism. Chronic racism and discrimination can lead to a wide variety of psychological problems, including denigration of one's sociocultural in-groups, feelings of helplessness, numbing, paranoid like guardedness, medical illness, anxiety, fear, and the development of posttraumatic stress disorder. (Hemmings, C., Evans, A., Identifying and Treating Race-Based Trauma in Counseling, (2018), Journal of Multicultural Counseling and Development, Vol. 46, Issue 1, 20-39IV). The importance of ensuring the highest level of training in anti-racism work, healing trauma work, and how white supremacy impacts the counseling profession, cannot be emphasized enough. **To have a workforce of counselors who are inadequately trained on these issues, can end up re-traumatizing clients, and will certainly increase mistrust in the counseling profession.** It is unethical and irresponsible to license counselors who haven't received training on the core issues addressed here. This is one of the most vital issues of our time. (Please see these important statements and articles:

Roberto Schiraldi

1. "APA Apology To People of Color for APA's Role in Perpetuating, Promoting, and Failing to Challenge Racism, Racial Discrimination, and Human Hierarchy in U.S." Resolution Adopted by the APA Council of Representatives on October 29 2021, 2. "Culture Centered Counseling", by Lindsay Phillips, Senior Editor of Counseling Today, ACA, November 22, 2021, 3. ACA Statement on Anti-Racism, by ACA Advisory Council, June 22, 2020).

17. Importance of counselors doing their own inner work on the effects of dwelling in a white supremacy culture, and its impact on our humanity. This is **lifelong learning** which requires a willingness to be vulnerable and continuing to discover, unpeel, acknowledge our implicit/unconscious biases, white fragility/ defensiveness/guilt. We were never taught this information, so how would we know. This is difficult, messy work. And none of us will do it perfectly. We will make mistakes. It's about acknowledging our mistakes, considering why it happened/where we learned it, apologizing when appropriate, and coming up with a reasonable plan to prevent a repeat, and then committing to carry through on our commitment. This is

what leads to real growth making us feel more confident if we persevere, with gentleness and compassion for ourselves and each other. It makes us much more likely to create trust with our clients from marginalized backgrounds.

(See these important books for doing inner work, 1. "How to Be An Antiracist", by Ibram X. Kendi, Random House (2019). 2. Diversity in Clinical Practice by Lambers Fisher, PESI Publishing (2019) 3, Promoting Cultural Sensitivity in Supervision, by Kenneth V. Hardy, and Toby Bobes, Routledge (2017) 4. Mindful Of Race by Ruth King, Sounds True (2018) 5. The Racial Healing Handbook, by Anneliese A. Singh, New Harbinger Publishing (2019) 6. "Me and White Supremacy", by Layla F. Saad, Sourcebooks (2020) and 7. "White Fragility", by Robin DiAngelo, Beacon Press (2018)).

18. Role of white supremacy cultural values leading to white privilege and racism. Understanding the intersection of white supremacy, racism, and white privilege. For example, when one group is "supreme" (from God's anointed ones, doctrine

of discovery manifest destiny), all other groups are not. This sets us all up for discrimination and racism. And, a supreme" group will automatically have benefits and privileges that other groups will not have...thus white privilege.

Bibliography: 1. *"What is White Supremacy"* by Elizabeth "Betita" Martinezwww.collective Liberation.org 2018. 2. *"No, I Won't Stop Saying White Supremacy"* by Dr. Robin DiAngelo Good Mens Project; August 12, 2018. 3. *"The History of Patriarchy"* by Ellie Bean Medium.com, November 11, 2018. 4. *'Post Traumatic Slave Syndrome'* by Dr. Joy Degruy, Uptone Press 2005. 5. *My Grandmother's Hands: Racialized Trauma and the Pathway to Mending Our Hearts and Bodies* by Resma Menakem Central Recovery Press, Las Vegas, NV, 2017. 6. *"White Supremacy Culture"*, by Tema Okun, Changework Racism Workbook, Oakland, Calif., 1999. 7. *"White Supremacy Culture"*, New Resolution, National Education Association Report, July 2018.

B. White Privilege

B. <u>White Privilege</u>

1. Definition of white racial privilege (and how it contributed to above sections I.A and B). Advantages and benefits people have because they are white (see list of benefits in McIntosh article cited below).

2. Definition of racism. Racial prejudices exercised against a racial group by individuals and institutions in a position of power.

3. Role of institutional power. (Internment camps for Japanese Americans as example of treatment of other marginalized groups).

4. Effect of "unhealthy" white heterosexual male values (superiority, power, wealth, control, elitism, entitlement, success, competition to be number one at all costs, defining beauty by European standards, etc.).

5. Internalized oppression of people of color. Accepting and internalizing stereotypes and myths exposed to.

6. Colorblindness. While seen by some as well-intentioned, denies the reality of existing racism.

7. What to do?

    a. It is important to acknowledge our privilege and take responsibility to speak

Roberto Schiraldi

out, support, and advocate, if there is to be substantial, sustainable change. This is not about guilt or shame; it is about acting. Complicit bias asserts "if we're not part of the solution, we're part of the problem".

b. **Teach core value that All life is Sacred -valuable, worthwhile, important, worthy of love, dignity, and respect, that all individuals have worth, regardless of grades, money, possessions.** This is a fundamental Native American teaching.

c. **Teach importance of Dr. MLK's speech, "I have a dream that my four children will one day live in a nation where they will be judged not by the color of their skin but by the content of their character."**

d. Demonstrate an on-going commitment to learning about and becoming comfortable with discussing White Supremacy Culture, White Privilege, Intersectionality Theory, Implicit Bias, Microaggressions and Broaching when appropriate.

e. **Appreciating the trap created by depending on a hierarchical notion of life. This limiting** paradigm labels cultures as "superior" or "inferior". In reality, human experience within culture cannot be placed in this hierarchy. Note the powerful concept of life as a circle rather than a pyramid. When counselors use the circular perspective, our work with clients is deeply transformed.

Bibliography: 1. *Teaching Tolerance/Teaching the New Jim Crow* by the Southern Poverty Law Center. http://www.tolerance.org/publication/teaching-new-jim-crow 2. *"Unpacking the Invisible Backpack"* by Peggy McIntosh, Wellesley College 1989. 3. *Teaching for Change. http://www.teachingforchange. org* 4.White Privilege Conference Course Curricula. NJ Dept. Of Education. Amistad Commission http://njamistadcurriculum.org 5. *The Great White Elephant: A Workbook on Racial Privilege for White Anti-Racists* by Pamela Chambers and Robin Parker. Beyond Diversity Resource Center, 2007 http://beyonddiversity.org/books, 6. *"Under-standing Internalized Oppression"*, by Teeomm K. Williams, Univ. of Mass. 2012. 7 *"Being Colorblind does not offset innate advantages of White Privilege"*, by Robert Jensen, Kansas City Business Journal, January 5, 2001, p.20. 8. *The Self-Esteem Workbook* by Glenn R. Schiraldi, pp. 29-37, New Harbinger, 2001. 9. *"A*

Journey through Alienation and Privilege to Healing," by Roberto Schiraldi, White Privilege Journal 2013. *http://www.wpcjournal.com/article/view/6457.*

C. Intersectionality Theory

a. Examination of factors of identity (gender, race, class, economic status, ability, sexual orientation, etc.), which intersect on multiple and often simultaneous levels

b. Recognition that people can be privileged in some ways and not privileged in others, and there may be limited awareness of one identity and not others

c. Multiple identities and systems of oppression at work and their impact on our counseling diagnostic tools

d. Importance of increasing awareness and not reinforcing deficit models of cultural groups.

e. Lack of experience in interacting with individuals from different groups can lead to over- or under-emphasis on cultural factors (**"Broaching"**).

f. Important never to assume, but to ask, if appropriate, about individual identities, (**"Broaching"**).

Bibliography: 1. *Race, Class, Gender: An Anthology* by Margaret L. Andersen and Patricia Hill Collins (8th ed. 2012) 2. *"Demarginalizing the Intersection of Race and Sex,"* The University of Chicago Legal Forum 140:139-167 (1989), by Kimberly Crenshaw 3. *Black Feminist Thought: Knowledge, Consciousness, and the Politics of Empowerment,* by Patricia Hill Collins. (2008), Messner, M. 'Unconventional Combat: Intersectional Action in the Veteran's Peace Movement', Oxford Press, 2021.

D. Implicit Bias

1. Definition. Prejudices that are unknown to the conscious mind, involuntarily formed, and usually denied. Developed over a lifetime through exposure to direct and indirect messages, early life experiences, the media and news programming. We all have them.

2. Examples of implicit bias (based on extensive research cited by Kirwan Institute below and Harvard University below, view and take IAT, Implicit Association Test).).

    2a. In emergency rooms, whites are pervasively given stronger painkillers than Blacks or Hispanics.

2b. Everyone is susceptible to implicit bias, even people who believe themselves to impartial or objective, such as judges.

2c. College student video game participants are more likely to "shoot" when the target is black.

Bibliography. 1. *The State of the Science: Implicit Bias Review 2013*, Kirwan Institute for the Study of Race and Ethnicity, Ohio State University, 2. IAT, Implicit Association Test, https://implicit.harvard.edu/implicit. 3. "Across *America, Whites Are Biased and They Don't Even Know It*", by Chris Mooney, Washington Post, (2014). 4. *"Blindspot: Hidden Biases of Good People"*, by Banaji, M., and Greenwald, A., Random House, 2013.

E. Racial Microaggressions

1. Definition. Everyday insults, indignities and demeaning messages usually unintentionally sent to people of color by white people who are unaware of the hidden meanings embedded in the communication.

2. Examples of microaggressions.

a. Myth of meritocracy which asserts that race, gender, class, sexual orientation does not play a role in life success.

b. "Color blindness" (Denying a person of color's racial or ethnic experience; the implicit message is "They should just assimilate").

c. Assumptions (Asian Americans and Latino Americans are assumed to be "perpetual foreigners;" or "inheritantly inferior", based on biased assumptions of intelligence based on race, gender, or perceived abilities).

Bibliography. "Racial Microaggressions In Everyday Life: Implications for Clinical Practice," by Derald Wing Sue, *American Psychologist*, pp. 271-286 (2007) 5. *Diversity and Oppression,* Graduate MSW Course taught by DuWayne Battle, PhD, Rutgers University/MSW Culture Competence Certification Program.

F. Broaching

1. Definitions. A consistent and ongoing attitude of openness with a genuine commitment to explore issues of diversity. Addressing and/

or responding to racially offensive comments, attitudes, and behaviors.

2. Examples of broaching styles:
   a. Avoids broaching. Regarded as unnecessary. Defensive when asked to broach.
   b. Broaches sporadically. Vacillates due to discomfort, lack of skill, and concern about negative reactions from others.
   c. Consistently broaches. Integrated and congruent with commitment to social justice.

Bibliography. 1.. *Broaching the subjects of race, ethnicity, and culture during the counseling process,* by N.L. Day-Vines et al, Journal of Counseling & Development, 85, pp. 401-409 (2007) 2. *Helping school counselors successfully broach the subjects of race, ethnicity, and culture during the counseling process,* by N.L. Day-Vines & T. Grothaus, ASCA Conference, Chicago (2006). 3. *Promoting Racial Literacy in Schools,* by Howard Stevenson (2014).

G. Non-violent Communication / Compassion Focused Therapy

1. Definitions. Non-violent Communication and Compassion Focused Therapy are two powerful approaches to assist us in learning how to give ourselves and others empathy and compassion as we address these often very painful issues.

2. Examples.

   2a. Work internally to acknowledge and feel compassion for own feelings and needs. Making a request of self. "Would I be willing to give myself respect, support?"

   2b. Express how I am to another without blaming or criticizing. "Would you be willing to help me understand what you're experiencing?"

Bibliography. 1. *Non-violent Communication,* by Marshall Rosenberg, Puddle Dancer, 2015, *Healing Across Differences,* by Dian Millian, Puddle Dancer, 2012, *Compassion Focused Therapy,* by Paul Gilbert, Routledge, 2010.

H. Healing From Racial Trauma

Definition - Race-based traumatic stress is an emotional injury that is motivated by hate or fear of a person or group of people as a result of their race, a racially motivated stressor that overwhelms a person's capacity to cope, a racially motivated, interpersonal severe stressor that causes bodily harm or threatens ones' life integrity, a severe interpersonal or institutional stressor motivated by racism that causes fear, helplessness or horror. Intersecting identities can result in multiple traumas and forms of oppression. Racial trauma can be viewed as intergenerational, that is, passed on from generation to generation, thus compounding the trauma.

Common reactions to Racial Trauma- shock, hopelessness, anger, numbness, rage, disbelief, grief, panic, preoccupation, guilt, ADHD, loneliness, overwhelming despair, flashbacks, uncontrollable tearfulness, fatigue, mistrust, high anxiety, low self-worth, increased use of alcohol and other drugs, headaches, pains, overeating, gastrointestinal disorders, hypertension, compromised immune system, pervasive sense of loss, and loss of feeling safe and others.

Approaches to Healing- Racialized Trauma Therapy should only be offered by well trained professionals who specialize in racial trauma and who have extensive experience and supervision in providing this support. Counselors who have not done been well trained and not done their own inner anti-racism work can re-traumatize clients. Feeling trust between client and therapist is essential and takes times to build. Racial trauma therapy can include acknowledging events, feelings, memories, being believed/ feeling heard and understood, having reactions and symptoms normalized, unburden family secrets, deep grief and rage work, rehearsing future safety measures, meditation, mindfulness meditation, keeping journal of self care / self-love practices, affirmations, acknowledging resilience and strength, spiritual practices, clear boundaries, accurate education, identifying needs like comfort, reassurance, compassion, respect.

Rage work - members of oppressed groups (including professional counselors and graduate counseling students), often need space to verbalize their rage at the countless injustices they have dealt with almost all their lives. For someone with no similar history, this is extremely challenging to witness and facilitate without rushing to tone down. This kind of emotion is also present in women & men who have been sexually abused.

Bibliography. key authors on the psychology of oppressed people: 1) Dr. Frantz Fanon. He crafted the moral core of decolonization theory as a commitment to the individual human dignity of each member of populations typically dismissed as "the masses". His book is a must read "Black skins, white masks" (1952). 2) Paulo Freire who taught us so much of what it takes to help clients who are persistently oppressed (his theory is "The pedagogy of the oppressed").\Freire, P. (1970). Pedagogy of the oppressed. New York, NY: Continuum. 3) Dr. Lillian Comas-Diaz, former APA president whose articles on the psychology of Latin women is fundamental to understanding how to work with women who come from oppressive circumstances in a way that affirm them rather than just deleting their symptoms. Comas-Diaz, L. (2006). LATINO HEALING: The integration of ethnic psychology into psychotherapy. Journal of Psychotherapy: Theory, Research, Practice, Vol. 43 (4):436–453. (2)Comas-Diaz, L. (2011). Multicultural approaches to psychotherapy. In J. C. Norcross, G. R. VandenBos, & D. K. Freedheim (Eds.), History of psychotherapy: Continuity and change (2nd ed., pp. 243–267). Washington, DC: American Psychological Association. 4) Scholar Dr. W.E.B. Dubois, Dubois, W.E.B. "The Future of the Negro Race in America." DuBois on Reform: Periodical-Based Leadership for African Americans.

Ed. Brian Johnson. Lanham: AltaMira Press, 2005. 160-171. He coined the construct of **double consciousness.**

Other Important Work on Healing Racial Trauma:

1. Bryant-Davis, T. (2007). *Healing requires recognition: The case for race-based traumatic stress.* The Counseling Psychologist,35,135-142., 2. Hemmings, C. Evans, A. *Identifying and Treating Race Based Trauma in Counseling*(2018), Journal of Multicultural Counseling and Development, Vol 46. Issue 1 20-39IV, 3. Telusma, B., *Do We All Have PTSD? Mental Health in an age of racial terror.* Grio, March 27, 2018, 4. DeGruy, J., *Post Traumatic Slave Syndrome,* Uptone Press (2005), 5. Menakem, R., *My Grandmother's Hands,* Central Recovery Press (2017). 6. *Scientific American, The Science of Overcoming Racism: What Research Shows and Experts Say About Creating a More Just and Equitable World.* Special Collectors Edition, Summer 2021. Volume 30, Number 3.

Summary. Acknowledging accurate history, and its connection to white supremacy culture, white privilege, racism, and intersectionality theory can assist us in understanding past and current racial struggles and pave the way to practice broaching and non-violent communication with our unintentional microaggressions, and the unconscious biases which may trigger them. With these understandings and internal work, counselors will be much more able to provide compassionate and supportive counseling for all their clients, especially those experiencing racial trauma.

© *2020 Schiraldi (Williams, Rodriguez)*

New Jersey Counseling Association Anti-Racism Statement *

November 2020

The New Jersey Counseling Association (NJCA) is committed to confronting racism in all its forms. This insidious disease of racism pervades all the systems of our country, including our counseling profession. Therefore it is essential that we each individually, and collectively as an organization, do our utmost to address this poison if we are to be most effective in providing the highest quality of care to each of our clients. We commit to uncovering, understanding and healing all vestiges of racism and white supremacist cultural values inside ourselves and our profession. We will do our best to seek out and provide the most effective education and training regarding anti-racism and white supremacy cultural values*, and their impact on all mental health and counseling issues. As individuals and as an organization, we will seek every opportunity to speak out against racism and white supremacy cultural values, and do our utmost to truly welcome and value All the People, especially those from marginalized backgrounds.

Roberto Schiraldi

*We believe that racism (in this country at least), exists as a result of dwelling in a culture of white supremacy.

This culture of white supremacy is a system that founded this country and still runs it. It is a system of power, wealth and control, where a predominantly few wealthy white heterosexual men are in power - a system where individuals are ranked as inferior or superior on the basis of race. In this system, all the racial groups, and all the other groups - women, LGBTQ, class, disabilities, and others, are cleverly manipulated and pitted against each other, each competing for equity and justice.

Understanding white supremacy cultural values such as power, wealth, control and elitism, helps us to see the hurtful impact on the marginalized, and on our common humanity. Using this understanding, along with a compassionate vision of courageous and loving action, provide a foundation for sustainable racial trauma healing and equity and justice for us all.

Therefore, NJCA is committed to directing our actions to the aforementioned for example, offering trainings, discussions, intentionality with planning yearly conferences (including connecting multicultural counseling content in training proposals). Additionally NJCA is committed to addressing white supremacy culture and racism for NJCA membership, and working to improve and increase multicultural counseling education and training requirements for graduate degrees and licensure.

Adapted from National Education Association Statement on White supremacy culture (2018)

American Counseling Association / Anti-Racism Statement

Jun 22, 2020

After discussion and discernment, the ACA Governing Council has issued the following statement on Anti-racism. The ACA leadership is listening to a cross section of members and volunteers in order to develop an action plan that will give life to this statement.

Racism, police brutality, systemic violence, and the dehumanizing forces of oppression, powerlessness, and White supremacy have eroded the very fabric of humanity which ideally binds our society together. Macrolevel systemic racism extends to disparities in institutional policies and procedures in physical and mental healthcare, education, the judicial system, employment, sports and entertainment, and the brutal violence of law enforcement. These larger societal oppressions lead to inaccessibility to resources and social marginalization, which descend finally to individual racist attitudes, implicit biases, stereotypes, microaggressions, and even death. The ongoing and historical injustices are not acknowledged by those who want to be in power or protect their entitlements. Some who do acknowledge, do so reactively, temporarily, or superficially and thus, no meaningful change occurs. Anti-Black racism is often reframed as accidental, an unfortunate incident, or as the criminality of the victim.

Words cannot truly capture our feelings. We are angry, exhausted, grieving, suffering, furious, and in despair. The American Counseling Association is pained by the murders of George Floyd, Rayshard Brooks, Ahmaud Arbery, Breonna Taylor, Tamir Rice, Eric Garner, Sandra Bland, Michael Brown, and countless other Black/African Americans who unfortunately remain nameless. We stand in solidarity with our Black siblings in denouncing the historical legacy and destruction caused by institutionalized racism and violence against Black people, perpetuated at the hands of law enforcement, the hatred bred of White supremacy, the deafening silence of dehumanizing and complicit inaction to address these systemic ills within our society. As counselors, we listen, we empathize, and agree with protesters that when absolute justice is established, peace will follow. Enough is enough, we cannot continue to watch fellow Black Americans being murdered, as the very life force is suffocated out of them.

The American Counseling Association is built on enduring values and a mission that promotes: human dignity and diversity, respect, the attainment of a quality of life for all, empowerment, integrity, social justice advocacy, equity, and inclusion. If we remain silent, and do not promote racial justice, these words become harmful and meaningless for our members and the counseling community. Given the rapidly evolving double pandemic of COVID-19 and the continued exposure of Black people to institutionalized racism, ACA wants to be clear about where we stand and the ongoing actions we will take. As proactive leaders, counselors, mentors, supervisors, scholars, and trainers we will break away from this structure of racism trauma, and the violence born on the necks of Black people.

Our stance is: Black Lives Matter. We have a moral and professional obligation to deconstruct institutions which have historically been designed to benefit White America. These systems must be dismantled in order to level the playing field for Black communities. Allyship is not enough. We strive to create liberated spaces in the fight against White supremacy and the dehumanization of Black people. The burden of transgenerational trauma should not be shouldered by Black Americans even though they have remained resilient.

All ACA members must be willing to challenge these systems, but also confront one's own biases, stereotypes, and racial worldview. Moving forward, our actions will be based on input from our members and the voices of others. We are committed to change.

Racial Justice Pledge

I pledge to continually learn about how this country was founded by and continues to be run by white supremacy values, such as power, wealth, control and elitism.

I pledge to continually remember how white supremacy cultural values hurts me, and our common humanity, and prevents true unity, equity and justice for all.

I pledge to continue to do my best to uncover, heal and change every vestige of white supremacy culture in me, and to support others in doing the same.

I will do my best to live with and share loving kindness and integrity in every thought, word and action.

I will seek and welcome every opportunity to work for unity, equity and justice for all.

Roberto Schiraldi

Initial Strategies For Engaging in Racial Justice Work

The following are offered as some preliminary suggestions when considering to do this very difficult, yet extremely rewarding work:

1. Educate ourselves through reading. Since we have not been taught this information it is our responsibility to continue to learn all we can. There are some initial essential books like, "The Fire Next Time" by James Baldwin, "How to be an Antiracist" by Ibram X. Kendi, "Between the World and Me", by Ta-Nehisi Coates, and "Tears We Cannot Stop" by Michael Eric Dyson.

    There is an ever growing body of literature, articles and books such as, "No I Won't Stop Saying White Supremacy"(article), "White Fragility" by Robin DiAngelo (book), "Me and White Supremacy" by Layla Saad (book), "Feeling White", by Cheryl Matias (book). "Waking Up White" by Debby Irving (book) There is an ever growing body of literature, articles and books such as, "No I Won't Stop

Saying White Supremacy" (article), "White Fragility" by Robin DiAngelo (book), "Me and White Supremacy" by Layla Saad (book), "Feeling White", by Cheryl Matias (book). "Waking Up White" by Debby Irving (book).

2. Educate ourselves through training. There are numerous training opportunities, didactic interactive, in person and on line. Some wonderful trainers and training organizations are:

Beyond Diversity Resource Center, beyonddiversity.org, Dr. Amanda Kemp (dramandakemp.com), Dr. Nathalie Edmond (drnatedmond@mmcounselingcenter. com, White Awake,(whiteawake.org), Peoples Institute For Survival and Beyond (pisab.org), Not In Our Town Princeton (niotprinceton.org). Training for Change (trainingforchange.org).

3. Do our best to integrate all information and experience. Am I willing to keep peeling away the layers for the rest of my life? How do the information and experiences touch me emotionally, mentally, physically, spiritually, socially, and how do I care for yourself well in all those aspects of myself. This is essential...

as the work can be very trying, to say the least. Pacing is huge. Engaging in counseling support with a specialist in multicultural counseling can be extremely helpful. And celebrating small accomplishments is huge. Consider making an ongoing commitment to do this work (see below).

4. Search for local ally groups, and do our best to establish trusting relationships with at least a few like minded individuals. This is also essential to have a supportive, sounding board to be vulnerable with and brainstorm and practice strategies. Consider supporting local Black Lives Matter groups.

5. Then, when we decide we are ready....choose to engage in "broaching"..i.e., addressing offensive behavior, always guided by first holding our self in the place of unconditional love and acceptance, and then holding the other in the place of unconditional love and acceptance. And being very gentle and kind with ourselves for being brave enough and caring enough to do this work, regardless of the outcome. Again...this is messy work, we will not do it perfectly, we keep on doing our best, with integrity, compassion and courage.

~

Justice Healing Meditation

Breathing In.....
Breathing Out.....

May we feel healing and peace...
May we share healing and peace.

May we honor our anger at injustice
and the terrible treatment of others.

May we use our anger for Loving Action.

May we honor our discomfort with lies

May we always do our best to speak with truth

May we treat ourselves and all others
with gentleness and kindness.

May we honor our tears for those who are suffering
and offer our comfort.

And may we re-member to walk gently upon this Earth
to honor our ancestors and our children....
so we All will be Free.

Roberto Schiraldi

Breathing In...
Breathing Out....

May we feel healing and peace..
May we share healing and peace.

Ah Ho. Let It Be So,
Mitakuye Oyasin (all my relations / all my relatives).

The following is an outline for a proposed organization in support of men coming together to support each other in learning, growing, healing, to become better men, and support our boys in becoming healthy men, in service of a better world.

Men for Racial Healing and Justice Proposal

Men for Racial Healing and Justice is an organization of men who are concerned about addressing racial healing and justice for ourselves and the world around us. While we males have made and continue to make so many positive contributions to our world, we are also, unfortunately, responsible for contributing to the vast majority of violence, oppression and destruction.

We believe that effective racial healing and justice must begin with us men holding ourselves and each other accountable and standing together to insist on racial healing and justice for us all. Safe, supportive environments are provided in which to do this most challenging and often painful work. With the support of other safe, strong, caring men, together we can heal ourselves and the world.

Roberto Schiraldi

Our mission is to continue to deepen our understanding of the white heterosexual male supremacy value system / how it has hurt us and our common humanity, and pitted us against ourselves and each other. This is the underlying, belief which drives our efforts. Fearlessly speaking this truth with love and action is our commitment.

Advocacy/Consultation/Individual and small group support

Providing individual and group support for stepping up and speaking out about racial justice. Exploring efforts to effectively interact with individuals and systems. Providing support for healing from racial trauma, and other related concerns.

Programs

A variety of programs are designed for organizations and institutions to explore the roots of internal and external racism and the ways to change ourselves and the world in ending racism.

Two Day - Four Day Intensive Gatherings.

"The Many Myths of Being Male: The Keys to Ending Racism".

These programs will allow for in-depth internal work and creating relational and team building opportunities as we peel away the lies that have oppressed us and hurt our common humanity. We will come away feeling refreshed and invigorated in our commitment to healing ourselves and ending racism.

Spiritual Healing Ceremony

Meditation and prayer circles
Sweat Lodges
Drumming Circles
Embracing the Quiet Within
Learning how to be compassionate with ourselves, each other, and our Earth Mother.

Program topics to include:

Growing up male
Stereotypes/gender role conditioning
Competition to be #1 at all costs (no matter who you need to walk over)
Power, wealth, control
Real strength / gentleness
Fear of Women (based on book by Wolfgang Lederer)
Fear of being vulnerable / the importance of honoring our emotions / how to be safe doing so

Archetypes: Hero, Warrior, King, Lover
Fatherhood
Friendship/brotherhood
Healthy relationships
Healthy Sexuality
Celebrating Maleness
Being impeccable with our word
Our Sacred Path
Our Sacred Nature
LOVE, what it really means, how racism is the lack of love, and how real love for ourselves and all life, is the antidote.

White Supremacy as Addiction/ Twelve Step Recovery

White supremacy can be viewed as an addiction, or powerful habit. This deeply ingrained habit injures the oppressed (as well as the oppressor) because it dehumanizes both parties. Continual denial about our internalized racial superiority often leads to habitual behaviors which are hurtful and feed inequity. For example, we may have automatic visceral reactions when we encounter someone of a different color. When we harbor unconscious biases towards others it is very difficult, if not impossible, to treat them fairly, compassionately or humanely.

When we have not been taught to carefully examine the internalized superiority of ourselves and our society, we will continue to perpetuate racism, even though we might say that we don't want to. It is a habit.

The Good News......like all habits, it can be broken.

The Twelve Steps of Alcoholics Anonymous and other Twelve Step Programs help to bring sobriety, balance and harmony, and to save the lives of millions of individuals. Applying Twelve Step principles can provide a helpful guide to addressing white supremacy. With brave, humble, and compassionate commitment to life long growth, we can free ourselves from this addiction, and discover the life of mutual love that we all deserve.

Twelve Step Recovery from white supremacy
(Inspired by the work of Dr. Gail Golden, EdD LCSW and others)

1. **We admit we were powerless over our white supremacy conditioning**
   – and that the lives of People of Color (and our lives), have been made untenable as a result.
2. **We have come to believe that doing our own inner work will restore us to sanity - and that freedom and balance can result from honesty about our history and our complicity. We cannot do this work alone, so we made a decision to seek leadership from People of Color.**
3. **We have made a decision to commit to life long learning and teaching about accurate history, and to uncover every vestige of white supremacy that lives inside us (especially the effects of "gendered racism"/ white male supremacy we learned from our founding fathers, and the harmful foundational values exemplified by the Doctrine of Discovery by god's anointed ones, Manifest Destiny, and the Constitution never**

intended for "all the people" ie., Indigenous People and Women excluded and Black People counted as 3/5 of a person, which all contribute to unconscious white superiority).

4. We make a searching and fearless moral inventory of ourselves, and how we are complicit with white supremacy policies and practices.

5. We admit to ourselves and another human being the exact nature of our wrongs.

6. We are entirely ready to learn from others who have effectively done this work.

7. We humbly ask for help from our Universal Consciousness*, from People of Color, (especially Women of Color), and allies who are willing to lead and guide us– being clear it is our responsibility to do our work and to always hold ourselves accountable, and be accountable to People of Color.

8. We make a list of persons we had harmed, and become willing to make amends to them all,

9. We make direct amends wherever possible, except when to do so would injure them or others – and only after clear understanding about our behavior, and well thought out

behavior changes and plans so as not to repeat the behavior.

10. We continue to take personal inventory and when we were wrong promptly admitted it (the truth will set us free)

This proposal is offered, with hope that all those in power (including you and me), will consider going back to the beginning, to boldly, lovingly, recreate a new vision for ourselves and each other. A Loving Vision of the Sacred... for Healing America...and our world. I offer you this, with hope and faith in our individual and collective commitment to living our lives with full love.... Being all we truly can be.

ALL LIFE IS SACRED

A Loving Blueprint
For Healing America

"I am poor and naked, but I am the chief of the nation. We do not want riches, but we do want to teach our children well. Riches would do us no good. We could not take them with us to the other world. We do not want riches. We want peace and love"

- Red Cloud (Makhipiya)
(late 19 century) Lakota Chief

Introduction: The Original Core Values

To Review:......While our Constitution espoused positive sounding values of liberty and justice for "All The People"... Women and Native People were excluded from the document, and African American males were counted as 3/5th of a person. Beautiful values and guiding principles of Love - honesty, fairness, kindness, compassion, generosity, respect.... were largely forgotten in the desperate quest for power, wealth and domination.

So in actuality, at it's core, the U.S.'s founding values were more indicative of fear, greed, hatred, material wealth, power and control, which further devolved to elitism, entitlement, superiority. "Success", was equated to competing to be #1, at all costs, no matter who we need to walk over to get there. Those initial values were derived by the misguided principles of "doctrine of discovery" by "god's anointed ones", justifying "manifest destiny". Those principles resulted in the genocide of the Indigenous People, the original inhabitants and stewards of the land, and the horrific inter-generational treatment of enslaved Africans upon whose backs our country's economy was largely built. Additionally, the careless slaughter of the animals and desecration of the land.... all for the use of those in power.

The aforementioned paved the way for protecting

those in power by establishing and justifying institutional core values of racism, sexism, homophobia, classism, xenophobia, ableism, ageism and on and on. So yes, we have many blessings, and of course, we also have many severe problems. So that's the quick and very dirty, explanation for the state of affairs we find ourselves in.

Now.....what do we do about it?

Choosing New Core Values To Live By:

All Life Is Sacred

Again, as I see it...the answer is really quite simple.... and yet....profoundly challenging. We each choose to claim, and live by, the incredibly powerful, core, loving principle.......“All Life Is Sacred”....Sacred...meaning worthwhile, important, valuable, precious, worthy of love, respect, dignity, awe and wonder. This also translates into this new perspective that I'm no better, no worse than that insect, the Land, that tree, that Woman, that child.....**ALL Life Is Sacred.** Once we live by the love principle, all of the poisonous “isms” would die out. The sacred inter-connectedness of all life...takes center stage..... we literally live by the idea of **“All interconnected, All One”**. This has always been a core spiritual principle. Now, the science of quantum mechanics demonstrates that at a cellular and molecular level, all of our cells and molecules are always changing and intersecting with all others. So we literally are, all connected and all one.

From the Lakota Native Spiritual Tradition... Mitakuye Oyasin (pronounced – mee tock o yay – o yah sin), meaning "All My Relatives, All My Relations, "We Are All Related...All One"...Each One my Sister, Each One my Brother....The Animals Are My Relatives... The Trees....All part of the Sacred Circle Of Life, The Sacred Hoop...Mother Earth, Father Sky, Grandfather Rocks, Wind Spirits, Thunder Beings....all Guides and Teachers from the Great Beyond....All To Be Honored and Cherished...and All to live with in Harmony. So I do my best to Be Grateful for the Sacred Gift Of Life, and for all the Gifts...My Relatives....and choose to release differences and judgments of myself and all others.

"Lose all differentiation between myself and others, fit to serve others I will be.
And when in serving others I win success, then will I meet the Buddha.
and we will smile"
-Milarepa, The Great Yogi of Tibet

"You will treat the alien who resides with you no

differently than the natives born among you; you
shall love the alien as yourself; for you too were once
aliens in the land".

- (NIV) Leviticus 19:33-44

So if this was the core guiding principle which drives the purpose, the vision and mission statements of every school and church, and all the other institutions in our country... and the world...imagine...please imagine.... the affect and effect on all of our children, and their children's children for the next seven generations to come......We will treat ourselves and each other with utmost gentleness, kindness honesty, respect, fairness. Because we are all in this together...we do not see anyone as an adversary in competition for a little piece of the pie. There is plenty to go around for everyone to have a high quality of life, when we choose to live with utmost mutual regard for the sacredness of all beings.

This is a system of values which is in **everyone's** best interest...individually and collectively. Of course, this would require a full-on **agreement**....and full-on **commitment**... by everyone. A **100% commitment** to being our best, with complete honesty and compassion in every thought, word and action, in how we treat ourselves and each other. A high bar to live by ....to be sure. And yet.....we would have soooo much to gain....

every one of us. And living by this guiding principle of the sacredness of all life creates this incredible opportunity for "**Loving** Thy Neighbor **As Thyself**". That's it. As simple as I can put it.

So now, a little more about this thing called **Love**.

Love

Since the beginning, all the wise ones have said …..Love **Is** the answer.

So, what is this elusive butterfly called Love?

As the inimitable Tina Turner sang…"*What's Love Got To Do With It?*"…….the answer……Everything!

The most powerful force in the universe is LOVE! Always has been, always will be. We humans just forget. And to be fair, it's mostly because we haven't really been taught about love……not nearly as we need to be. The word is thrown around so carelessly, most often without really even knowing what we mean by it. "*It's just a feeling….can't really be explained…. but you know it when you feel it*"……like that. Talk about bogus. We've been brainwashed, bamboozled, hoodwinked……to desperately seek this ….thing…… that we can't even describe……and we wonder why so many relationships with ourselves and each other end up not feeling fulfilled. As the wise and

courageous activist and writer bell hooks (lower case, her preference) so heart-fully teaches us in her wonderful book "All About Love".....we need to define the core values of love (my words, not hers), and then we can create lives filled with those values. Values like gentleness, kindness, commitment, integrity, courage, vulnerability, dependability, fairness, compassion, understanding, responsibility, respect, gratitude, trust, and being willing to support ourselves and each other in our mutual spiritual growth. Spiritual growth, for me, implies a life-long learning adventure in deepening my inter-connectedness with all other life, so that we may best serve all others.

So we're not talking about mamby pamby, goo-goo, ga-ga fantasy love, we're talking about the real deal.... fierce, active, passionate, clear, on solid ground LOVE. And it has to start with us being taught about how to honor, and cherish, respect, and care for **ourselves**. And holding ourselves to the highest and most honorable standards of human decency and fairness. If we are willing to bravely venture into this adventure in learning how to love ourselves....and to share that with others as we grow......which, to me, is the main purpose for our being born,.....then all good things are possible.

So there you have it sports fans! That, to me, is the essence to our living harmoniously with ourselves and each other, on our Sacred Mother Earth. The question then becomes...if we agree, in principle about the aforementioned core values of the sacredness of all life, and of living in love as the blueprint for honoring the sacred....then what are we willing to do about it?

For me it's all about the powerful word......"COMMITMENT". Am I....Are You....Are We....each individually...and collectively......ready..... willing.....and able to commit to living our lives in beauty...walking the Sacred path of Love....in all of our thoughts, words and actions.......... ...individually and collectively? If we are....we can fix the problems we've co-created.....if we are not.....then we will continue to have the unfulfilling existence we have. Again, commitment, to me, means....100%...all in... not 99%....for that 1% will sabotage our best efforts. That doesn't mean we will do it all perfectly...that's not the point. It's that when we mess up, which we will.... no big drama, no excuses.....just, pick ourselves up, dust ourselves off, look honestly and humbly at what we missed that created the misstep, acknowledge it, come up with a better strategy for fixing it expediently, and then carry through with a sustainable plan. In Twelve Step Programs we call it taking a fearless and searching moral inventory and making amends, and committing to and following through on real change. This is similar to the Truth and Conciliation process which so many individuals, families, communities, nations have used to great avail. (Please refer back to some of my prior poems and pieces on truth and conciliation if you're interested in reviewing a little bit more about these and other similar, complementary processes).

I don't know about you...but I'm ready, willing and able to commit to co-creating the amazing life here, and around the world, that I believe we were all put here to live. I hope and pray, that you are too....and that is why you are still reading this.

Real love is humble, and gentle and kind, courageous, and impeccably honest. The following are guides to live by, to create inner well-being and outer well-being for us all. So let's look at some of the core ingredients of love and what they represent, (at least to me). And as we explore these core values more and more, it becomes clearer how they each intersect with and complement each other:

"Out of the Indian approach to life there came a great freedom – an intense and absorbing love

for nature; a respect for life; enriching faith in a Supreme Power; and principles of truth, honesty, generosity, equity, and brotherhood as a guide to relations".

-Luther Standing Bear (1868-1939)
Oglala Lakota chief

So let's look at some of the core ingredients of love and what they represent, (at least to me)

And as we explore these core values more and more, it becomes clearer how they each intersect with and complement each other:

Core Love Values

Courage- The willingness to lean into the difficult challenges of life, to Be, and to Do the "right thing". Even in the midst of others' disapproval. A great guiding question for any quandary in life is...."What would love do now?" "What would be the most loving thing I can do for myself in this situation....that little still voice of truth inside, will always guide us home.....to love....if it doesn't feel right, then the guide isn't love, it's usually fear or guilt. Really important to keep re-learning about that distinction. Are we willing to be courageous enough to be vulnerable...with our feelings....this is the mark of a true love warrior.

Honesty- A strong promise to ourselves to act and speak with authenticity. No white lies. When we "get over" on others we're really getting over on ourselves. No way we can feel good about ourselves without living honestly. "The truth **will** set us free". Which is why it is so essential to live by this core value. Lest we be imprisoned by our secrets. "We are as sick as our secrets" (from 12 Step Principles).

Integrity- Living with a strong sense of justice and fairness. We live congruently....our behaviors match our values. And again, a willingness to speak up and take action when we see or feel inequity and injustice. Living with impeccable honesty and integrity frees us to live in peace with ourselves, and to feel a deep sense of respect and acceptance.

Kindness - We treat ourselves, and others with gentleness, compassion, generosity, empathy, understanding, support. Again, it is crucial that our relationship with ourselves is based on utmost kindness. Otherwise our treatment of others, will likely fall short, and ring hollow, eventually, even leading to resentment and sabotage.

Are thoughts and actions reflect our desire for the well-being of ourselves and all others.

Commitment - We consistently follow through on our promises to ourselves and others, especially when the going gets tough. And with all these, when we fall short, no big drama, no beating ourselves up, compassionately acknowledging where we went wrong, and revising strategies that are perhaps more realistic and more sustainable.

Dependability - We do what we say, and say what we do. Similar to integrity. We believe and have faith in ourselves, because we carry through on our commitments...first and foremost with ourselves, and of course also with others.

Responsibility - We take pride in being accountable to ourselves, first and foremost...honoring our most important love priorities in self-care, and the care of others. Being responsible for our well-being fills us with a sense of contentment and peace, since we know we are "taking care of business". Having clear boundaries is very important. If we don't know what our limits are, and don't honor them, we can become resentful, and being doing things out of guilt and fear, not love.

Fairness/Equity/Equality – We treat ourselves and others with a sense of fairness, equity and justice. We do our best to ensure equal and fair access to life necessities for all, economically. food, clothing, shelter, educationally, healthcare...a desirable quality of life for all. If one of us is suffering, it hurts our common humanity. Again, there is plenty to go around if we live by fair and just standards.

Patience and Acceptance – We do our best in all of our thoughts words and actions to be very patient with our imperfections, and to hold ourselves and others with unconditional positive regard. We do our best to check our judgments of ourselves, to treat ourselves fairly. And we strive to do the same with others, by trying to put ourselves in their shoes. While this can be extremely difficult....like with all of these values, it can also be extremely rewarding, as it gives the best chance of interconnecting with others who may seem different than us.

Trust - Trust takes time to build for ourselves and others. When we consistently demonstrate over time, that we are trustworthy, that is true to our word, then trust becomes a great gift we give ourselves and others. When trust is broken, this is how we determine our willingness to recommit to our core principles. We can do this by carefully accessing what let to the break in trust, and what needs to happen to regain the trust for ourselves and the other. A sincere, heartfelt amends, when appropriate can be very helpful. And then following through on well-thought out strategies to make things right for ourselves and with others (ideally, vetted by the injured party). And of course, consistently carrying through on our commitments to change, and monitored over time. If need be, reassessing and altering strategies as needed.

Respect – Treating ourselves and others in the way we would like to be treated. Being respectful and considerate of our and others' feelings, and needs, as consistent with our core values of love and sacredness of all life. Respecting all boundaries, especially sexual ones. Treating ourselves and each other with dignity and reverence for each one's worth. This can be especially difficult when there is significant disagreement, Yet, most disagreements can come to fair and equitable resolution, if both parties are committed to treating each other with respect and kindness, and a willingness to meet in the place of equity and fairness.

Gratitude/Affection – Wise elders often say that gratitude is one of the most important love values there is, and can be a true source of genuine affection which we all so greatly need. Affirming and acknowledging our self care, along with our gratitude to the other, can be beautiful and heart filling gifts which make a huge impact on our mental, emotional, spiritual, physical and social well-being.

And relationships individually and collectively can prosper and grow through this simple act of loving expression.

Spiritual Growth - Willingness to nurture spiritual growth in self and others - When we choose to believe in and live by a belief in the core worth of ourselves and others, and of our inter-connectedness to all things, then our life becomes a reflection of that core value, by how we treat ourselves and each other in our daily lives. Decision making about the most simple, and the most difficult challenges becomes more achievable as our confidence grows through the experience of our spiritual growth.

Roberto Schiraldi

Core Love Values Inventories

Using the Core Love Values Listed Above, please consider filling out the following two Core Love Values Inventories For Self and Others, and for Leaders, Institutions and Organizations. For the second inventory, you might start out by picking one leader, institution or organization that moves you to want to take action, and see what comes up for you. (Institutions and organizations may include any groups such as schools (especially teaching accurate history), healthcare, wildlife, environment, churches, business, police/prisons (of course would include treatment of inmates), military, government (especially promoting truth and conciliation processes), and others. In service of all the people, all leaders, institutions and organizations would optimally be reviewed internally and externally (perhaps by unbiased, carefully selected, civilian review boards) for realistic compliance and sustainability on an annual or bi-annual basis. And, for example, a mailer could be sent to cross sections of the state populations or townships asking for feedback using the inventories for whichever leaders institutions/organizations are up for review. Feedback could then be summarized and used for regular review and planning sessions. Citizen ownership would then be a vital, ongoing, mutually advantageous process. Data from both inventories help us determine what is working, and improving what needs improving. This is not about being adversarial with ourselves or others, it's about working together for optimal outcomes for all

Roberto Schiraldi

Core Value	Rate how treat self/others from 1-10(10 being optimal) Self/Others	Describe recent time demonstrated that value Self / Others	Describe specific plan to improve that value Self / Others
Courage			
Honesty			
Integrity			
Kindness			
Commitment			
Dependability			
Responsibility			
Fairness/Equity Equality			
Patience/ Acceptance			
Trust			
Respect			
Gratitude/ Affection			
Cooperation/ Service/Sharing			
Spiritual Growth			

All Citizen's Core Love Values Inventory For Self and Others*

*Based on Fearless and Searching, Kind Moral Inventory from Schiraldi, G. R. (2011), *The Complete Guide to Resilience: Why It Matters; How to Build and Maintain It.* Ashburn, VA: Resilience Training International. © 2011 Glenn R. Schiraldi, Ph.D. Not to be reproduced without written permission** *Human Options.* Toronto: George J. McLeod Limited, 1981, p. 45.

All Citizens' Core Love Values Inventory For Leaders, Institutions, Organizations*

Core Value	Rate how leader treats employees and public from 1-10 (10 being optimal)		Rate how Inst./Org. treats employe/pub. (from 1-10)		Describe recent time demonstrated that value		Describe specific plan to improve that value	
	Emp	Pub	Emp	Pub	Leader	Inst./Org.	Lead.	Inst./Org.
Courage								
Honesty								
Integrity								
Kindness								
Commitment								
Dependability								
Responsibility								
Fairness/Equity Equality								
Patience/ Acceptance								
Trust								
Respect								
Gratitude/ Affection								
Cooperation/ Serv./Sharing								
Spirit.Growth								

*Based on Fearless and Searching, Kind Moral Inventory from Schiraldi, G. R. (2011), *The Complete Guide to Resilience: Why It Matters; How to Build and Maintain It*. Ashburn, VA: Resilience Training International. © 2011 Glenn R. Schiraldi, Ph.D. Not to be reproduced without written permission** *Human Options*. Toronto: George J. McLeod Limited, 1981, p. 45.

Roberto Schiraldi

Tree Of Living Love

The following is a visual representation of the Tree Of Living Love – a symbol of the mutual commitment to live and nurture ourselves and each other... All life. One way to view this is to envision a truth and conciliation process, that is, speaking the truth about our history, and seeing it all, through the eyes of a gardener and the garden of life. We live in a beautiful garden. There are many gorgeous flowers and plants of all colors and shapes. There are also invasive and aggressive weeds that may look attractive, however, left unattended, may drain the soil of it's nutrients, and overpower and suffocate the natural healthy and balanced growth of all of the flowers and plants. It may be noted, that the poison of some of the weeds, blended with the sweet pollen of some of the flowers and plants, can have powerful healing properties. So the gardeners need to first learn about and recognize the poisonous roots of decay. And then the garden needs continuous, vigilant weeding and tilling and revitalizing of the soil to maintain the precious life affirming balance.

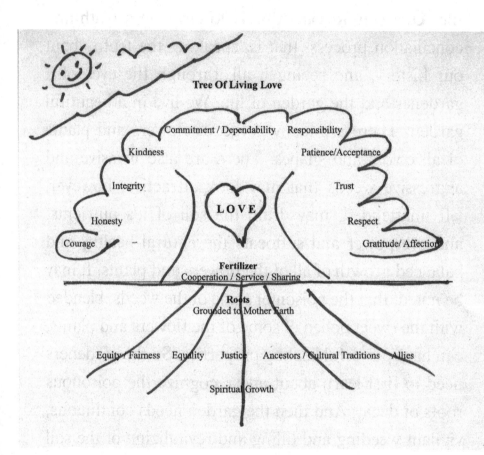

Tree Of Living Love

Commitment / Dependability   Responsibility

Kindness   Patience/Acceptance

Integrity   Trust

LOVE

Honesty   Respect

Courage   Gratitude/ Affection

Fertilizer
Cooperation / Service / Sharing

Roots
Grounded to Mother Earth

Equity / Fairness   Equality   Justice   Ancestors / Cultural Traditions   Allies

Spiritual Growth

Commitment Proposal

It is proposed, that every citizen will sign and commit to live by the following agreement(whether born here or not... refugee, immigrant, young, old, gay, straight, parent, child, blue color worker, white color worker, educator, government servant, police/ peace keeper, business person,...and on and on)....in other words, everyone of us.

All Citizens' Agreement*

I, as a citizen of this Country, of this World, as a representative of ...All The People....Pledge my life, to do my best with every thought, word and action... to make choices based on the core belief that All Life Is Sacred, and that each choice will reflect core Love values by:

1. Checking and accessing my commitment with each core value as listed
2. Expressing each value commitment out loud to myself, and ideally to another I feel responsible to
3. Continuing to reassess my commitment of my pledge to myself and the others I serve,

through regularly scheduled written and spoken self-reflection

4. Committing to maintain regularly scheduled, mutually agreed upon reviews with those I serve

5. Signing my name as my promise to live by each value

This is my word.

Signed

(It is recommended that a yearly day of celebration be initiated to honor every citizen's living by their sacred pledge).

~

The Creator, Great Spirit, Wakantanka, The Universal One, never fails to remind me of the sacred, loving path, and the ongoing work to restore balance.

- My cherished teacher of the Lakota traditions, Tom/Rags sent two beautiful passages to me about the importance of the two-spirited ones (who embody the greatest qualities of the sacred feminine and sacred masculine, all in one), and who are beautiful, healing empaths for us to turn to for wisdom, healing, guidance.
- Another grueling, agonizing pipeline protest by brave Indigenous People and their supporters, to prevent further illegal desecration of sacred lands.
- **My beloved friend and brother John invited me to accompany him in support of some distinguished Lakota Elders who are part of a delegation traveling east to retrieve the remains of Lakota children who died at one of the first Indian boarding schools. The children had been forced to leave their families and tribes (to be "assimilated", "kill the Indian, save the man"), often treated horrifically, many never seeing their loved ones again. Their families and tribes had been previously prevented from taking their remains home. Now, over a hundred years later,**

they can be brought home. The wounds so deep...
so deep. Yet, finally, maybe now, their spirits can
be free. And a little healing can start.

For a moment....if you would.....please take a deep
breath...close your eyes... and try to imagine how you
would feel... in your heart and body.... if one of these
children.... is your child.

Roberto Schiraldi

The Children

Oh... the Children.
their spirits
yearning to be free.

Finally they can return
home again
to their loved ones.

And their spirits
can continue
on their sacred journey.

Honoring Our Children
.....from the plantations
.....from the boarding schools
.....in the border detention centers
.....in human trafficking
All of our children, everywhere
For seven generations to come.

All children want to know..
Am I loved?
Will I be comforted?
Is the world safe?
The answers determine

a kinder world.

In saving our children,
We save our country.

In saving our children,
We save our world.

In saving our children,
We save...ourselves.

Honoring the children
through loving action
is how we can re-create
a loving world.

Mitakuye Oyasin
All My Relatives

Please keep the spirits of the young ones, who have suffered so much, in your loving hearts and prayers ..... their families and loved ones, ... the elders who continue this difficult healing work.... and all those who work to make it right.

~

"When the first chakra is disconnected from the feminine Earth, we can feel orphaned and

motherless. We look for security from material things. Individuality prevails over relationships, and selfish drives triumph over family, social and global responsibility. The more separated we become from the Earth, the more hostile we become to the feminine. We disown our passion, our creativity, and our sexuality. Eventually, the Earth itself becomes a baneful place. I remember being told by a medicine woman in the Amazon, "Do you know why they are really cutting down the rain forest? Because it is wet and dark and tangled and feminine"
- Alberto Villoldo, Ph.D,
Dance of the Four Winds: Secrets
of the Inca Medicine Wheel.
(With loving appreciation, once again, to my dear friend and colleague Dr. Maria del Carmen Rodriguez, for sending the above quote to me, and for her loving help with editing this essay.)
~

Please see "America Needs A Woman President", by Brett Bevill, drawings by Eben Dodd, a wise and moving little book which really gets to the heart of our huge need for more Women in leadership positions, especially Black, Indigenous, LGBTQ2S,

and Women of Color, who live and lead by the core
sacred love values previously discussed.

~

"I am going to venture that the man who sat on
the ground in his tipi meditating on life and its
meaning, accepting the kinship of all creatures, and
acknowledging unity with the universe of things,
was infusing into his being the true essence of
civilization."

Luther Standing Bear (1868?-1939)
Oglala Lakota chief.

~

~

"You might say I'm a dreamer,
but I'm not the only one.
I hope some day you'll join us,
And the world will be as one"
-"Imagine"
John Lennon

~

Roberto Schiraldi

Dear Ones,

May our heart-felt choices
to share our love with each other,
be the healing we all so long for.

May we each cherish
the Sacred in us,
and all things.

May we each walk
in love and beauty,
as we make our way
back home again.

Roberto

This little breathing meditation is offered to soothe and comfort whatever pain or discomfort you may be feeling. Please use whatever variation feels most nurturing for you. (It is drawn from Mindfulness Meditation Practice of Jon Kabat Zinn).

Healing From Pain

Breathing...

In... out.

Deep... slow.

Calm... ease.

Smiling... releasing.

Present moment... wonderful moment.

Breathing....

(releasing all judgement and criticism)

...honoring thoughts... returning home to breath...

...honoring all feelings...returning home to breath...

...honoring all sounds...returning home to breath...

...honoring all sensations... returning home to breath...

...always gently returning to the Breath.

...scanning our entire body...

...from head to toe...(or toe to head)

...bringing gentle awareness to each part of the body...

...through the breath... tending to each part of the body...

...always gently returning home to the breath.

Heart of the Pain Soothing Mediation

Placing our hands over our heart.......creating a slow, nurturing rhythm.....

...I breathe in slowly....soothing, comfort...

...gradually.....deepening... to the heart of the pain.

...I lovingly embrace and become one with the pain...

...soothing, comforting breaths of tender healing...

...Breathing out, I release all pain and discomfort...

...(Breathing in and out, deeply with each affirmation)..

...Each cell is a spark of Sacred healing that creates a chain reaction of life, strength and vitality...

...I am enfolded in Universal Healing Light...

...My blood flows unobstructed through every artery and vein...

...My blood flows free and easy through every artery and vein...

...I release all pain to Universal One's loving hands...

Roberto Schiraldi

...Breathing in, I am calm, comforted, soothed...

...I breathe in Universal soothing light..

...My heart is enfolded in Love...

...My heart is enfolded in White Light...

..My head is clear...by heart is healed... I am soothed and comforted.

...May I be free from pain and suffering...

... May we all be free from pain and suffering...

...All Is Well...

...I Am Love...

...All Is Well...

...I Am Love.

Closing and Hope

I wish each of you all the beauty and wonder of this amazing life.

I hope you decide to care for yourself with strong and gentle... love.

May your service to others be a reflection of that strong and gentle love.

Author Contact Info

Should you wish to contact me, you can find me through my web site....www.robertoschiraldi.com.

I have been interviewed for a number of racial justice related podcasts, which can be found on my website.

There you can also find information on how to order two abridged audio books recorded in my voice (each approx. two hours long), one on Healing Love Poems for white supremacy culture, and the most recent one, on 'Healing from the Trauma of Macho-ism'.

Printed in the United States
by Baker & Taylor Publisher Services